CALLED TO ACT

CALLED TO ACT

5 Uncomplicated Disciplines for Men

VINCE MILLER

EQUIP PRESS

Colorado Springs

CALLED TO ACT

Published by Equip Press, Colorado Springs, CO

First Edition: 2020
Called to Act / Vince Miller
Paperback ISBN: 978-1-951304-27-0
eBook ISBN: 978-1-951304-28-7

DEDICATION

To my wife, Christina Lynn Miller, who makes me a better man every day.

To my two sons and daughter, Riley Jackson, Grant Jonathan, and Faith Savanna. May you be great men, may you find a great man, and may you raise great men.

To Mark Wylie, who generously allowed me to use his home in Maui as a place to focus and write this book.

To my Board of Directors for believing in me, supporting me, funding me and projects like this; for believing that it is possible to build better men.

To every leader of men out there who has stuck with it and grinded it out on behalf of men. We may feel like a disorganized movement, but I want you to know you are supported. Your investment is valuable. And God is glorified when you gather men for his purposes.

CONTENTS

INTRODUCTION

So, what makes a great man?

I have pondered this question for most of my life. Most days it is my first waking thought: *What does it look like to be a great man, husband, father, and leader today?*

Yet most days I feel like I'm missing the mark. And I suspect most men feel this way.

When we consider the exchanges we have had with our wives, our kids, and people in general, we're often disappointed at the missed opportunities. We look back over moments we could have been more thoughtful, moments we should have been more understanding, and times we could have been more intentional. Each day we long for a way to become a better man—a better husband, father, and leader. And sometimes we need someone to point us the way.

For me, that man was my grandfather. By the time I met him, he was retired from the Navy and had lost his hair, but I still knew him as a strong, hard-working man. He was the son of an Oklahoma farmer. He played golf daily and drove a sweet 1959 red Chevy Apache truck. He was generous, loving, patient, and disciplined. And most of all he loved Jesus Christ. The origin story of my relationship with Christ is really a story about my grandfather and all the times he mentored me in that fire-engine red truck.

He was the man that taught me to be a man, because men were otherwise absent from my life. My bio-dad left when I was two years old, and my stepdad left when I was fifteen. After that, there was a lot more time with Grandpa. And because he invested the time, my life was changed. It wasn't overnight, but rather a little at a time. His influence changed me forever.

He taught me how to be a real man by following one man–Jesus Christ.

When I was twenty, he died. Cancer got him. He tried to hide it from me, but we all knew for years it was eating him alive. Through an act of generosity, someone paid for me to head home from college to see my grandfather again. The ticket got me home in time to spend one final hour with my grandfather before he died. Lying in his hospital bed, with all the energy he could muster, he engaged with me in a final conversation. The conversation was really about trivial things. Girls. College. Work. And of course, the truck. Neither of us said anything profound, but it was still deeply meaningful to me, one of the greatest memories of my life. Divine moments are sometimes nestled within trivial conversations. As the pain increased, he spoke his last words, "I need to rest now," and we both knew what he meant. His time on earth was done. The next few hours I sat at his bedside quietly waiting for him to die, and I listened to the ambient noise of him gasping painfully for each breath. Eventually the breaks between the gasps for air grew farther and farther apart until his life was gone.

I will always remember that day. It was a life-changing moment. I felt by confronted by a new reality. In that moment I heard the call God placed on my life. It was as clear as day. I prayed a prayer out loud that went like this:

> *"God, for the rest of my life, I want to do for other men what my grandfather did for me—mentor men."*

That was 30 years ago, and I am still living out that covenant with God. I continue to do my best to faithfully pass on to others what my grandfather passed on to me.

The Purpose of this Book

My purpose in writing this book is to answer a question that I think bothers men today. And here is the question:

- *God calls us to take action, but how do we become that kind of man?*

It's really a two-part question.

- *What does it mean to be a man?*
- *How does one act like a man?*

It's a great question if you think about it. To embrace your identity as a man, you need to know how to define manhood; then you need to move from this definition into real action.

I think it is critical not only to ask these questions but to have clear and simple answers. I want to be able to attain the goal of being a great man, but I also want to be able to confidently teach my children and others what a godly man looks like. In this way, I'm passing on what my grandfather passed onto me.

Take a look at this touching moment. King David, one of the greatest leaders of all time, is about to die. He is handing the leadership baton to his son Solomon; listen to what he says.

> *"I am about to go the way of all the earth," he said. "So be strong, act like a man."* 1 Kings 2:2

Over the years I have dug into this topic from many different angles. I've found that defining manhood can be a complicated task. And what complicates it are all the different approaches men use to define and attain their identity. Here are some familiar approaches.

First, some choose to define manhood by contrasting it with womanhood. Men will reinforce this contrast by using phrases like "man-up" and "don't be a sissy," which have a long-standing negative connotation for women. Even subtle expressions of this contrast do not describe manhood. They may reinforce our ignorance about the definition of real manhood, since many of the attributes of manhood and womanhood are remarkably similar.

Second, others tend to describe manhood by contrasting it with childhood. You will hear some men make proclamations like "grow up" or "don't act like a baby–man up." But these are failed attempts, too.

While this contrast might appear to gain ground, it fails to account for the magnificence of childlike innocence, youthful receptivity, and even the faith that Jesus appreciated in young children. Such a definition of manhood is focused exclusively on maturity: physical strength, accrued knowledge, and emotional stability. Yet we cannot ignore the fact that while these are good and important traits for men; we should not outgrow some childlike attributes.

Third, there are some who choose to define manhood based on a role or position in life. For example, manhood as defined by the position of husband, father, or occupational title. Now, here we might feel like we are getting somewhere. But we must pose the obvious question, *"Am I less of a man if I am not married, have no children, or don't have a job?"* While on my journey of becoming a man I will always need some direction on how to navigate the challenges of these roles and positions, but I believe our definition of manhood should transcend them.

Finally, there are still others who might define manhood as something achieved through positive virtues or avoidance of vices. Now, we *do* make more progress with this approach. For evidence we turn to one of the great works on this subject, Aristotle's *Nicomachean Ethics.* His study on this topic has influenced our thinking on manhood and masculinity for more than two thousand years. It is the greatest work of its kind. Aristotle encourages men to pursue virtue or moral excellence through our own effort and internal motivation; he says we should each direct our own development, motivated by our own self-interest and our desire for the praise of men. While virtue needs serious effort and attention, for the God-fearing man, strength comes from God himself through the power of the Spirit, not from self. We should be motivated by the love of God, not the praise of men.

There may be other approaches some men use. But if we pursue these paths we will fail in the pursuit every time because culture, comparisons, or pursuit of masculine virtues do not define or make a man. Masculinity is merely a social construct, and social constructs are ever changing.

It's God alone who makes man and defines manhood.

It's God alone who makes man and defines manhood.

It is God who made the original man at the beginning of time, as well as our new model of manhood–the man named Jesus Christ. In Christ we have God's answer for what it means to be a man. God himself provides the model for man and manhood in Christ, who demonstrates exactly what this looks like in action. Man is defined by living in complete submission to the will of God. In Christ, we discover everything that the first man could have been had he had not chosen to live independent of the will of God. Christ is the model, perfect in all ways.

There is your answer to the first question. What does it mean to be a man? Answer: Jesus Christ, the man of God fully submitted to the will of God.

But the second question is perhaps more difficult to answer. *How do I act like a man?*

Well, this answer may appear complicated, but it's not. And regardless of our answer, it must be simple if we are going to get men to act. If you have scanned the outline of the book, you've already seen the answer. To act like a man, you must only do two things:

Hear and ***act***.

How we do these two activities for the entirety of our lives is the central concern of this book. Part One focuses on **how we hear** as a man. Part Two focuses on **how we act** as a man of God. And I hope this will become so uncomplicated for you that you will embrace this teaching for the rest of your life.

This is a book for men, on becoming a man. It is for anyone who desires to know how to become God's man. It's for your son, brother, father, uncle, nephew, and cousin. It's for men to give to the men in their lives. It's for women to give to men. It's for men young in their faith and even men more advanced in years. It's for small groups of men and for those engaged in one-on-one mentorship. In the end, this book contains everything I have learned during my daily endeavor to become more of the man God wants me to be. And I pray it will help you as well.

PART ONE

The Search for a Man Who Acts

1

The Search for a Man

The Story for Men and About Men

Since the beginning of time God has been looking for men to lead. In fact, you are that man. God has given you tremendous resources: power, dominion, authority, voice, and even a moral code to lead out in faith.

God's quest for a man capable of leading goes back to the dawn of time. God handcrafted us in his image. By his own hand he crafted man, gender male, and designed us by his hand with his own image in mind for us; what an honor! There had to be a reason for God to create us so thoughtfully; he must have created us with intent. From the creation of Adam God was looking for a man who would represent him, live by his values, stand tall in faith, love him completely, and steward all that he had created.

But the story of man takes an abrupt turn. All came crashing in when he and woman ate of the fruit from the tree that God had outlawed. In an instant a perfect world was stained by sin. And when God inquired of man as to what had happened, he blamed the woman that "God gave him", and in turn he did the unthinkable–he blamed God. And the story of sin and blame echoes down through time.

Today, men still neglect to act, just as Adam did. Nothing has changed. More often than not we are as passive in the face of temptation today as we were in the garden. We ignore the important and vital commands of God. We blame circumstances or others for our failures. We fail to take action and stand up and speak up for what is right. And at the root of it, we suffer from the disease of apathy. But there is a solution. There is hope.

The Issue Bigger Than Sin

Sin is definitely a problem for men. It's a big problem: one we try to fix but soon discover we can't. And Christ is the only one with a solution for sin, so he has chosen to make it his problem to solve on our behalf. Yet we can be tempted to use our freedom from the curse of sin as license to be apathetic toward sin. But we still have a battle to fight. We need power, and our God, the one of second chances, knows this. He offers us not only the salvation we need, but also the subsequent power to fight our war against the apathy that continues the cycle of sin.

Freedom from sin is not a license to be apathetic

God never intended or designed man to be apathetic, but rather to take action. In the garden, even before the corruption of sin, he gave man power, dominion, and authority in creation. He gave man meaningful authority and work. He even gave him voice to name and define all creatures. And God spent time with him in the evenings, walking and talking about creation and life. I wonder what this must have felt like. Can you imagine the freedom, the power, the authority, the work, and the unhindered relationship with the living God?

And with all this, man was burdened with only one boundary–a single rule.

"You are free to eat from any tree in the garden; but you must not eat from the tree of the knowledge of good and evil, for when you eat from it you will certainly die." Genesis 2:16–17

He wasn't given a rulebook, or even ten commandments. Instead he was given just one moral boundary: a clear commandment not to eat of one designated tree. Within this specific delicious-looking fruit, God placed supernatural powers. Isn't it interesting that God chose the activity of eating, something we do with regularity, as the first moral boundary and also the means of supernatural power?

Soon after granting all this responsibility, God allowed something to brew inside of man: desire. For an extended period of time, he allowed man to live alone. Now, although God was present, a desire for something natural and human surged inside of man. Man felt the desire for companionship and relationship of a human nature. And in a rightly ordered way, God fulfilled this desire for man by providing for him woman. The story of mankind is off to a great start, but a dilemma is introduced in the very next chapter of life.

In Genesis 3, everything takes a turn for the worse. Woman is in the garden, talking to a serpent. (If this scene is hard to imagine, think about that talking gecko we've all seen on commercials.) So woman is engaged in conversation with this serpent, which seems to her a natural, nonthreatening occurrence; it's probably a conversation she has had many times before. The woman, persuaded by the serpent, takes of the fruit, brings it back to man, and then they both eat. The boundary is demolished, and sin enters the world. They do the one and only thing that they were commanded not to do–they eat from the forbidden tree.

And while man may raise a finger and point to woman for everything she did wrong, notice man's role in this incident: inaction. Remember, man was given power, dominion, authority, oversight, meaningful work, voice, and one moral rule before woman was created. Given all these resources, you would expect to see and hear something from man as he operates within this state of great power and authority. But apathy is insidious, deceptive, and cunning. It is man's great issue. Man does nothing and says nothing in the face of injustice and sin, even though he was empowered with everything needed to speak up and stand up.

Man does nothing and says nothing in the face of injustice and sin, even though he was empowered with everything needed to speak up and stand up.

Mind you, this was not the serpent's fault, it was not man's wife's fault, and it definitely was not God's fault—even though man attempted to blame them all. It was man's fault—my fault, and your fault. Man, gender male—that's you and me—has allowed apathy to cloud his thinking; our inaction has launched a once-perfect world into a place of perpetual pain.

Here is the lesson learned: the strategic place to begin our journey as God's man is dealing with the flaw of every man—our apathy. That apathy led to the first sin and sin thereafter, but we can fight against it in partnership with a God, who defeated sin for us and with the Holy Spirit who empowers us for the ongoing battle.

God's Search for A Man

The entire Bible is a story about God's hopeful search for a such man, a man who will engage in the conflict with apathy. A man who will speak up and a man who will stand up and act. One who will resist the impulse of apathy that lies within every man's heart.

Throughout the Bible we discover many hopeful men who fought boldly against apathy. We often tell their stories but fail to notice what inspires us about them: they were willing to do what we often will not. Their words and actions tell a story of the defeat of male-pattern apathy. They give us a glimpse into what God's man, a man of action, looks like. None of them were perfect. They were still fallen men with their own apathetic moments, but each one gives us hope: hope in whom we can be when we act as men of God.

Abraham

Abraham was one of these men. Abraham is known as the "father of faith" and the "father of nations." This identity stays with him throughout the Bible. Even today he is frequently identified as an example of what it means to live faithfully as a man, husband, father, and leader. He is a man who cashed it all in, leaving his homeland and all its comforts to follow God to a land he had not seen and knew nothing about. He was given nothing except a single mandate by God, and in faith he pulled up the tent stakes, turned to his wife, and said, "We're going." God called, and Abraham responded, "I'm all in!" even when he had no idea where he was going. He had no directions, no step-by-step map, no G.P.S., and no idea of the challenges he would encounter along the way. The impulse of apathy often convinces a man to rely on the routine and cling to current comforts. Not Abraham. He saw well beyond the apathy of the moment into God's vision for his future.

The book of Hebrews says this about him:

> *"By faith Abraham, when called to go to a place he would later receive as his inheritance, obeyed and went, even though he did not know where he was going. By faith he made his home in the promised land like a stranger in a foreign country; he lived in tents, as did Isaac and Jacob, who were heirs with him of the same promise. For he was looking forward to the city with foundations, whose architect and builder is God."* Hebrews 11:8–10

We learn a lot about Abraham from this short account of his life. Abraham did what some men would never do. He did it because he knew God's vision for his future was greater, grander, and better than his present small, limited, and myopic view. Abraham gives all men a glimpse of the man we want to be; of the man God wants us to be, a man whose vision is God's vision, not compromised by human reality and impossibility; a man who responds to his call and acts in faith, not paralyzed by fear; a man who holds a long view and does not let short-term concerns deter him; a man who focuses on identifying and taking the next step, rather than worrying about the gap in the distance between the present and the future; a man who will remain committed to a God-sized reality no matter how long it lies beyond his view.

Who doesn't want to be more like Abraham? And he is just one of many all-in men. There are more.

Moses

"Since then, no prophet has risen in Israel like Moses, whom the Lord knew face to face." Deuteronomy 34:10

Moses is one of the greatest leaders of all time. He was known as "Israel's teacher," a man who saw God face-to-face. It was his leadership ability that put him on the map of great men who fought against apathy. He led the greatest migration of people in the biblical record. He led them out of 400 years of slavery into freedom while preparing them for a new life in the land that God promised, where they would become the nation of Israel. But the task was not easy. Moses repeatedly confronted the Pharaoh and his Egyptian military forces—and he had to mutually convince 1 to 3 million leaderless Israelites, with whom he had no prior relationship, to follow him across a sea and into a desert. Laughable! How about that for a leadership challenge? Sign me up! (Not really. I take my family of five on vacation and I'm exhausted.)

We learn a lot from Moses about what it means to be a man: how to confront the demons of our past, how to deal with conflict, how to trust God when our life is on the line, and how to act faithfully even when we don't know the outcome. Through Moses we learn how to teach when we feel we lack voice. It is because of Moses and his leadership and teachings that we have the first five books of the Bible. Yet before he could become such a hopeful man, he had to win his own battle with apathy.

In the following text, even as Moses is speaking with God, we hear a little bit of uncertainty in his voice. We hear a man that wants to waver and give in to apathy—but we know he won't. He will instead become a hopeful man, one who stands tall in the narrative of scripture as a man of God.

"So now, go. I am sending you to Pharaoh to bring my people the Israelites out of Egypt." But Moses said to God, "Who am I that I should go to Pharaoh and bring the Israelites out of Egypt?" And God

said, "I will be with you. And this will be the sign to you that it is I who have sent you: When you have brought the people out of Egypt, you will worship God on this mountain." Moses said to God, "Suppose I go to the Israelites and say to them, 'The God of your fathers has sent me to you,' and they ask me, 'What is his name?' Then what shall I tell them?" God said to Moses, "I AM WHO I AM. This is what you are to say to the Israelites: 'I AM has sent me to you.'" Exodus 3:10–14

David

And finally David, among men, was unique. Twice in scripture he is labeled "a man after God's own heart."

"After removing Saul, he made David their king. God testified concerning him: 'I have found David son of Jesse, a man after my own heart; he will do everything I want him to do.'" Acts 13:22

David is the ultimate man's man. He was everything a man would want to be. An underdog from the start and the youngest of eight brothers, God selected him, anointed him, and appointed him to be leader over the nation of Israel. He became known as a warrior, poet, musician, lover, friend, king, and leader of the 40 mightiest warriors to ever walk planet Earth. He charged alone into war with a giant, inspired a nation, and wrote majestic psalms that bring men to tears. Today David still gives men hope not just for a new life of courage and faith, but for a vibrant relationship with God. Like David, we can valiantly battle against our apathy.

Every Man Fails

Each of these men failed. Each had an epic fail that became part of their story and thus a permanent black mark on their record. Just like you and me, they blew it–and in a big way.

Abraham failed when he told King Abimelech that Sarah (Abraham's wife) was actually his sister, fearing that the locals would be so smitten by Sarah's beauty that they would murder him to make her an eligible bachelorette (Genesis 20:1-3). Moses failed when he tried to provide water for the Israelites by striking a rock twice in anger rather than speaking to it, as God had instructed him (Numbers 20:9-12). And David failed by staying home when he should have been at war. Instead of leading his soldiers, he spied from the roof of his palace one of the wives of his 40 mighty men and decided to sleep with her. Worse, David then ordered the murder of his loyal warrior to cover up his sin and make the woman permanently available to him (2 Samuel 11:1-5).

But we should not be surprised by the failures of these great men, since every man fails. No man is invulnerable to failure. We cannot escape it. Failure is our greatest teacher. You might even be reflecting right now on some of your failures—some known only to you. Failure weighs on the conscience of all men, but you are in good company! You are in the company of great men who also had great moments of failure. But God teaches us the greatest lesson: a life of self-reliance and self-righteousness exposes our greatest apathy—the failure to rely on the power of the living God. Through each failure comes another opportunity to hear and act differently than before. Each failure is another moment for confession, repentance, forgiveness, restoration, and action against the previous apathy. The lesson is not that men (that's you) are a failure. You may feel this way, and sound bites from others around you may reinforce this, but you are not a failure. You are simply a man created in the image of God who has had a moment of failure. It is through our failures that God wants us as men to become more reliant on him so that next time in that moment of apathy we turn to him for the needed strength.

So what does it look like to stand against our apathy? Here are a few common areas where men tend toward apathy—with predictable results.

The Failure of Anger

> *Everyone should be quick to listen, slow to speak and slow to become angry, because human anger does not produce the righteousness that God desires.* James 1:19–20

I believe most men struggle with some form of anger. Anger–when it is poorly understood and unchecked–leads to failure. Anger is destructive in relationships at home, work, school, and on the field of play. This is true whether anger expressed or suppressed. Our anger leads some to shout, scream, and swear in an effort to forcefully attain justice for a wrongdoing or to regain what we perceive as control over the situation. For others it leads to buried thoughts and feelings that develop into relational bitterness that can affect men silently for years.

Many men, regardless of how they express or suppress anger, wrongly believe anger is the only socially acceptable masculine emotion. Movies sensationalize male anger, vengeance, and retribution, which leaves us feeling a strange form of short-lived personal relief. Yet under it all we do experience other emotions. We just don't believe that society finds them acceptable. And while scripture is clear that it's acceptable to become angry, unmoderated responses to anger lead to unproductive results. When anger spurs in us the impulse to act, it is good and healthy we simply need to select productive responses worthy of our calling.

A man needs keen awareness to fight this battle with apathy. He should understand that his anger is unique. It's challenging to navigate. Although we should not succumb to apathy, not every circumstance requires the same response. There are occasions in which we experience a personal injustice that will require patient self-restraint. Jesus called this "turning the other cheek" (Matthew 5:38). Remember, this is not apathy: it is well-placed right action. On the other hand, there will be occasions when it will be right to respond to injustices against God or others; here we are called to speak up and act out for righteousness in a proper way. Jesus modeled this when he entered the temple courts and proclaimed, "Get these out of here! Stop turning my Father's house into a market!" (John 2:16). Discernment is the key. We must correctly identify both the injustice at play and the appropriate, non-apathetic response. Anger can therefore cause problems for us when we allow it to override the decision-making process.

As men we need to discover the right responses to anger in each and every moment it emerges. And we also need to acknowledge the other emotions at work within us. We are not one-dimensional emotional creatures. There are other acceptable emotions buried deep underneath our anger like hurt, sadness, and grief. We must recognize these and other deep insecurities during moments of anger if we wish to guide our words and actions down righteous paths. We must learn to understand the emotions we feel, understand how they hijack the decision-making process, and learn how to lead and guide them in a way that honors and reflects God's will, not our own. This is the non-apathetic man. A man of hopeful action.

The Failure of Pride

> *The Lord detests all the proud of heart. Be sure of this: They will not go unpunished.* Proverbs 16:5

Pride is man's archrival. We are, after all, legends in our own mind. You know this is true.

Frequently we generalize our prideful tendencies; it is often too painful to identify specific debacles when we let pride get the best of us. We are sometimes apathetic toward these tendencies because pride is like a drug to our under-acknowledged soul. Simply put, pride makes us feel good when we are down. We get a rush from it every time; it's invigorating to a man desperate for attention. Sometimes we need a bump of pride so badly that we fault-find and criticize others. We conceal pride from others by being superficial and defensive. We pursue pride by looking for attention and overlooking others. Either way, in the end, we fall flat on our face.

Men must battle with the apathy that gives pride free rein. We must actively pursue our new identity as a servant, subject to the humility of Christ. Each day we should serve others and look for ways to take action against our prideful impulses. If we are apathetic toward pride, it will spread like a virus, infecting our mind, feeding our ego, and affecting our actions. Pride is always lurking, ready to influence our behavior if we let our guard down. Every day we have to make a decision to submit to Christ instead. Failure to engage in this battle against pride makes our defeat inevitable. The non-apathetic man stands on his guard, acting daily in opposition to the quiet voices of self-affirmation.

The Failure of Lust

> *"But I tell you that anyone who looks at a woman lustfully has already committed adultery with her in his heart."* Matthew 5:28

Lust is challenging for men. For many of us it may be the most persistent challenge. And while this may feel like a new problem because of the modern prevalence of pornography, lust has always been an adversary. It's an old problem.

So our underlying problem is not access to pornography, the acceptance of pornography, or even our hyper-sexualized culture. The problem is a desire issue within a man's heart. We are apathetic in addressing our lustful desires. And it's not a problem resolved simply by human effort or the removal of the object we objectify. The issue is that we fail to redirect the desires in our heart.

The hard truth is that men struggle with lust because we prefer to do so. We prefer to feed physical desires, and we desire the subsequent physical and temporary relief. And we choose to passively submit to our physical desires because we have not discovered the satisfaction of desiring something more beautiful and biblical. I promise you, the short-lived endorphin release you get from lustful indulgence is nothing compared to the satisfaction of knowing Christ and finding your desire in him. Christ is simply more satisfying; completely satisfying. A hopeful man knows this, understands this, and lives in this daily—satisfied not by lust but satisfied in God.

The Failure of Greed

> *It teaches us to say "No" to ungodliness and worldly passions, and to live self-controlled, upright and godly lives in this present age.* Titus 2:12

Finally, we face the pleasures of this world and its temptation for more and more and more. Greed feeds more greed, until finally we are living an out-of-control life. All men crave excess; when we get a little taste of something good, we naturally want more. Envy and greed are like twins from the same family of sin. The difference between envy and greed is that greed is a strong desire for more and more possessions like wealth, power, and significance, while envy adds fuel to the flame by fixating on what our neighbors have. Men who are greedy often lack empathy and real connection to others, objectifying people and things. We become apathetic toward the interests of others. In turn we think only of our own self. A greedy man has few real friends. He is reduced to only the people he knows who have something he needs. He is a transactional man.

But a godly man understands when enough is enough. He is not apathetic toward greed; he says no to its aggressive advance in life, stopping the progression of greed before it turns to envy and the objectification of people.

In the end, none of us escapes from all of these failures. None of scripture's great heroes did, either. From Adam to the present, failure has been a constant in every man's life. Yet we don't have to passively and apathetically stand by in the presence of failure. In fact, God has something very different in mind.

The Search for a Man Ends

> *"I looked for someone among them who would build up the wall and stand before me in the gap on behalf of the land so I would not have to destroy it, but I found no one."* Ezekiel 22:30

In the book of Ezekiel, we see God is serious about his search for a man who will "stand before him in the gap." Here, God has failed to find one willing man. But he continues to search today. What kind of man is he searching for? Well, he is looking for a man who both hears and acts. A man who will stand with God in a time of need when apathy is prevalent.

The God who empowers men is looking for a willing servant. In Ezekiel's day, who did God find? No one. The question remains: Who will be God's man?

God's Provision

I wonder if God gets mildly irritated with man.

I know this is probably not true, but doesn't it make you wonder?

Following God's lamentation in the passage from Ezekiel, he would go on to present a working solution—God himself provides such a man. In this self-provided man is one who hears and acts as a man should. It's God's choice, after all; this being is both divine and human, the one who hears and acts in the way God intended. This man came with power, dominion, authority, voice, and an unassailable moral code. He is the ultimate man. He is the "Son of Man." And this man shows all men how to be a real man. His name: Jesus the Christ, of Nazareth.

From the moment of man's first failure in Genesis 3, God knew his self-provided choice would be the solution.

> *"And I will put enmity between you and the woman, and between your offspring and hers; he will crush your head, and you will strike his heel."* Genesis 3:15

There are five more predictions in the first five books of the Bible about his choice of man: Genesis 9:27; 12:2-3; 49:8-12; Numbers 24:15-19; and Deuteronomy 18:15-18. In the rest of the Old Testament, there are hundreds more predictions that provide hope by pointing us to the end of the quest for a consummate man. God enabled the search and was also the solution. Although it often appears he was hopeful for mankind, God knew the solution all along. Through God's self-provision, we get the prototype for all men—the second Adam, the rebirth of man.

Failure is Necessary for Grace

While we think all this failure may be a bad thing, it gives way to something incredible. Our failure is imminent and inescapable; it's a product of being born into a fallen world. And while God does not want us to repeat failure, each time we fail we learn another way not to do something. Failure is also definitively better than doing nothing—which is utter apathy. We beat ourselves up over failure. We should not. Rather, we should appreciate that failure allows us to experience the most important part of our journey of becoming godly men: God's gift of grace, which fuels our return to battle against apathy.

Failure is definitely better that doing nothing and saying nothing in the face of injustice and sin.

We need God's grace to become God's man. Reliance on this grace is what empowers us to carry out our battles against apathy. This grace is most needed and best understood in our sin, suffering, and brokenness. Men live in a world of earning, deserving, and merit that reinforces our human deficiencies. As we fail, we sense the judgment of others, the punishment for wrongdoing–and worse, we judge ourselves. Thus, real men are made through God's grace. Judgment destroys men; grace strengthens men. Gentlemen, we need grace! Even more grace, and grace upon grace. But not to abuse its power–rather to work hard in cooperation with it to become the men God designed us to be.

Real men are made through God's grace, provided by one man–Jesus Christ.

Grace is getting what you don't deserve from God and simultaneously not getting what you do deserve from God. Grace is what only Christ can provide; it comes on the heels of every tragic failure. Through grace we receive four things that will change a man's life.

Men Find Identity in Grace

For it is by grace you have been saved, through faith—and this is not from yourselves, it is the gift of God—not by works, so that no one can boast. For we are God's handiwork, created in Christ Jesus to do good works, which God prepared in advance for us to do. Ephesians 2:8–10

Men will easily find their identity in any available thing that communicates value. Our annual income, our ability, our accomplishments—as these things go, so goes our identity. That is, unless we find our core identity in something better, more stable, and far more secure. And for God's man, our identity is not found in a thing but in a relationship. God "hand-crafted" us, and like any designer, God has an intent and purpose for his design. In God we find everything we need for living out our identity. His design and gracious redemption are the work of his hands. They are reminders of our need for dependence on him and reminders that we find our identity not in the things of this world, but in God alone. Our identity is found in God's grace and no thing else.

Men Find Confidence in Grace

Through whom we have gained access by faith into this grace in which we now stand. And we boast in the hope of the glory of God. Romans 5:2

A man fueled by God's grace discovers God-confidence, not self-confidence as the world teaches. Again, it's not a thing that gives us confidence; it's a person—God. God gives us confidence to act when we feel an impulse for inaction or feel beaten up by sin, which is the ultimate reminder of failure. With grace we have nothing to lose, since grace demands that we recognize we have already lost. We need confidence in God's salvation to take another step. In grace we live like a winner, enjoying the victory over sin that Christ won for us. Our pride and confidence come from him, not from things of this world. We stand in confidence because we know God is going to get all the recognition while our failures are forgotten.

Men Find Our Means of Action in Grace

Now this is our boast: Our conscience testifies that we have conducted ourselves in this world, and especially in our relations with you, with

> *integrity and godly sincerity. We have done so, relying not on worldly wisdom but on God's grace.* 2 Corinthians 1:12

If you are looking for right conduct, integrity, sincerity, and wisdom, all these are powered by grace. Rather than finding strength in personal ingenuity, we rely on God's wisdom. His wisdom, conveyed through scripture, is our means of action. We act according to his words. Obedience is powered by God's grace. Whereas before we were hopelessly falling flat in sin, with grace we will still fall–and then dust ourselves off again, knowing we get another chance. And another. And still another–infinitely–but we now rely again on his wisdom to act a little differently, one step at a time. Apart from God, we can do nothing, but with God anything is possible. It is God's grace that purely powers our means of action.

Men Must Receive Grace to Become a Man

> *For if, by the trespass of the one man, death reigned through that one man, how much more will those who receive God's abundant provision of grace and of the gift of righteousness reign in life through the one man, Jesus Christ!* Romans 5:17

Finally, grace is the means of becoming God's man. It is strange and unusual, but it is the only rite of passage into true manhood. Most cultures across time and geography have made use of rites of passage. People have long understood that without clear markers on the journey to manhood, adolescent males have a difficult time making the transition and will drift. Thus, rites of passage were identified in nearly every culture as one of the community's most important practices for young men.

Grace is the only rite of passage into true manhood.

While almost every culture has a rite-of-passage ritual, there exists a great diversity in what each one looks like. The common thread has historically been an experience that involves emotional and physical pain and requires a boy to pass the test of manhood: a show of courage, endurance, and the ability to control his self.

While these virtues (courage, endurance, and self-control) are important, the Christian rite of passage drives deeper to the core of man's issues. A Christian man's rite of passage is not about self-sufficiency, but rather complete and total dependence. We aren't supposed to achieve independence, but rather fully submit in dependence on Christ. After all, he is the man who makes it possible for us to become true men. Our only rite is this–the full acceptance of grace that results in full dependence. When a man learns to trust the power of grace he becomes less apathetic toward God and his ways, and thus becomes God's man. This is an ongoing ceremony that all men must embrace daily, not just one time. We must learn the way of grace to travel the road of a godly man.

You Are the Man Christ Is Looking For

> *Then Jesus said to his disciples, "Whoever wants to be my disciple must deny themselves and take up their cross and follow me."*
> Matthew 16:24

God wants men to be adventurous and courageous. He wants us to lay claim to being men. We are the men of God's choosing, and we must take up the call and charge. It is you God wants; the way forward is not easy, but it's full of grace and adventure. As Jesus said, just "follow me."

2

Man Is Called to Listen

A Man who Listens to God

"Honey, did you hear me?" said my wife.

Of course, I did, I said in my head. *Now what was that again?*

I bet that never happens to you. Your wife, boss, friend, or relative says something but you were so absorbed in your own thoughts or so distracted by work, a game, or something on TV that you literally heard nothing. Not a word. You might even have responded, but you don't recall a word she said.

Superficial and distracted listening is a challenge in any relationship. I am guilty of it daily. I miss critical moments in a conversation because I am not really giving my undivided attention to the conversation, email, lecture, or meeting happening right in front of me. And while we can get away with some of this in human relationships, it can be catastrophic in our relationship with God. One of Jesus's well-known parables, the Parable of the Sower, addresses this very issue.

> *On another occasion Jesus began to teach by the lake. The crowd that gathered around him was so large that he got into a boat and sat in it*

out on the lake, while all the people were along the shore at the water's edge. He taught them many things by parables, and in his teaching said: "Listen! A farmer went out to sow his seed. As he was scattering the seed, some fell along the path, and the birds came and ate it up. Some fell on rocky places, where it did not have much soil. It sprang up quickly, because the soil was shallow. But when the sun came up, the plants were scorched, and they withered because they had no root. Other seed fell among thorns, which grew up and choked the plants, so that they did not bear grain. Still other seed fell on good soil. I came up, grew and produced a crop, multiplying thirty, sixty, or even a hundred times."

Then Jesus said, "He who has ears to hear, let him hear." Mark 4:1–5

I love every careful word and action of Jesus here. He puts himself out in a boat to create an outdoor amphitheater experience for the gathering crowd. In doing so he ensures that everyone–I mean everyone–can *hear* him. With the sound ever so crisply echoing across the water, he commands their attention with the shout, "*Listen*," and then closes his storytelling with the statement, *"If you happen to have ears, then pay attention to what I am saying because it's important."* That's a paraphrase, but you get the point. He is saying you'd better *listen up*. And the story at the center of his lesson punctuates how well men listen. Jesus makes use of familiar farming metaphors to ensure that everyone understands him, since everyone in that day farmed at some level.

How could anyone miss the point of his story? Well, they did then, and still do today.

Listening to the Soil and Seed

When Jesus invoked the image of a farmer scattering seed onto a field, every person listening to the story would have known the imagery, and they also would have been familiar with the four types of soil on which the seed fell.

The path is the property boundary. As the designated place where people walk, the ground is hardened and pressed down. It's so hard that the scattered seed remains on the surface and does not seep into the earth and so become food for the birds.

The rocky soil is culturally distinct, since Israel's topography looks a giant limestone exploded over the countryside. The visible rocks serve as raw material for walls and boundary markers, but some remaining limestone is hidden just inches under the surface. The top of the soil appears fertile right up until the heat warms the sheets of limestone just inches under the surface. This bakes the roots of any new sprouts, destroying the seed shortly after it peeks above the soil.

The thorny soil is familiar soil. It has potential for results, but the soil is home to a predator–weeds. These thorny weeds choke out the good seed and its full potential. The seed splits, sprouts, and grows, but can't produce because it never comes to full maturity.

The good soil, in comparison to the other three types of soil, actually produces. And the results are unthinkably prolific.

The crowd surely perked up at this point in the story. Thirty, sixty, and even a hundred-fold yields? These are unbelievable results. But remember, Jesus isn't giving a farming lesson; he's teaching a spiritual lesson about what it means to be a follower who *listens.* It's not a story about farming at all, but about the results of effective listening.

The Four Ways Men Listen

Jesus was helping us to understand four ways that men listen and the result of each. In this story, the type of each soil represents a level of human receptivity–the essential effectiveness with which we listen. *The seed* represents the truth, and not just any truth, but *the* truth–God's truth. *The farmer* is anyone who sows God's truth, which (in this moment) happens to be Jesus (but the farmer of the story could represent any truth-teller). The ultimate point of the story is to emphasize the power of one particular way men listen by first telling us three ways we don't.

The path represents a man who is *unwilling to listen.* Remember, the truth is being scattered or shared, and he *does* hear it, but he refuses to act. He could be uninterested in the pursuit of truth, believe his own truth is the only truth, or simply be unwilling to relinquish his current position and perspective. In the end he is unreceptive to truth's call. The fact that he chooses not to act shows us that he did not listen.

The rocky soil represents a man who *initially listens.* With great initial enthusiasm, he hears the truth and has some early receptivity. Maybe the truth has elicited an emotional response; he hears and demonstrates initial action, but he does not persist by making continued action regarding the truth; as a result, when the enthusiasm wears off, his obedience withers and dies.

The thorny soil represents a man who *partially listens.* But this man's predators are all the other competing things he's hearing that prevent him from hearing only God's truth. As a result, this man chases after other apparent truths–not just *the* truth. His pursuits restrict and prevent truth's full growth in his heart, so although he hears a little bit longer than the last man, and even acts on it a little bit, over time the other competing ideas pervert and stunt the growth of God's truth. In the end, right action is prevented again.

The good soil represents the man who *fully listens.* This man is fully receptive to God's truth and in the end he is the only man who produces anything. Jesus makes special note that the receptive man is greatly productive because he both *hears* and *acts* upon the truth of God.

While listening is the successful integration between hearing and acting, there is another level of listening integrity that Jesus is after here. It's not just listening: we must hear, and act, and *also* become motivationally receptive to allow the truth to act on our desires. This motivational integrity is not simply behavioral integration between our hearing and acting, which can result in pretending and hypocrisy, it's hearing the truth, allowing it to affect our human desires, and then acting accordingly. From here a man produces visible evidence that results in thirty, sixty, or even a hundred times what is expected. Truth has now taken root not just in our behavior alone, but deep in our soul.

Motivational integrity is not simply behavioral integration between our hearing and acting, which can result in pretending and hypocrisy, it's hearing the truth, allowing it to affect our human desires, and then acting accordingly.

I have come to realize over the years that we are quick to categorize ourselves according to these soil types, selecting one as the best match for our nature. While there might indeed be a definitive match, we are more likely to share traits with all of these soils at the same time. For example, we may be hard, rocky, thorny, and even receptive of God's truth delivered by a particular person in a particular way, all at the same time. At one moment we may be highly receptive to certain types of truth, presented by certain types of people but when these situations are slightly altered, we become increasingly resistant. When we are highly receptive; we hear and act fully. But some truths are harder for us to accept. Depending on the matter, we may listen *initially* before returning to our previous position, *partially* without making the wholesale changes the truth requires, or we may be *unwilling* to listen at all. In these cases, we will produce less than desirable results. Honestly, the truth can feel inconvenient to us at times. It might require challenging spadework, removal of large rocks, and even some weeding; sometimes we are less receptive because the response demands harder work than what we are willing to endure. All men encounter this challenge. There are going to be circumstances and relationships in which we resist God's truth because of the effort required for us to live out that truth.

The Rite of Christian Manhood

But here's the thing: while grace is the means of manhood, listening is the evidence–it's our rite of passage.

Listening is our rite of passage into Christian manhood.

Many cultures across human history have tried to effectively capture the attributes, virtues, and behaviors of manhood. Some cultures have even developed elaborate ceremonies (called rituals or rites) for young men who are coming of age. The Christian male's active rite of passage into manhood is marked not by a ceremony, but rather by his ongoing receptivity to God's truth and is evidenced by his faithful response. When we act in submissiveness to the teaching, rebuking, correcting, and training provided by Jesus and his truth, we exhibit evidence of Christian manhood. Our *"ceremony"* is daily receptiveness and responsiveness to the truth of God.

All Scripture is God-breathed and is useful for teaching, rebuking, correcting and training in righteousness. 2 Timothy 3:16

We must train daily in our pursuit of godliness. A righteous man is willing to hear the truth and to act with immediacy. Hearing plus action, or *listening*, is our rite; it's our evidence, our indication of ongoing maturity. Many mistakenly believe that we naturally achieve maturity at a certain age or level of experience, that at some point we'll passively gain the ability to act according to God's truth. Not so! Obedient action that daily affects the heart is evidence of maturity, not the other way around. Our receptivity and response to God's grace and truth is the only rite of passage into Christian manhood and maturity.

In the end, the real problem with men is we are motivationally unreceptive, evidenced by our poor listening. And we partially listen in one of a few ways.

Denial

Again Peter denied it, and at that moment a rooster began to crow. John 18:27

This situation closed an unfortunate chapter in Peter's life. The man who said he would never deny Christ had done just that. Not once, not twice, but three times—even as Jesus had said he would. This was not Peter's finest moment, but sometimes men respond this way when we are cornered and confronted. Denial is a defense mechanism; it's a response to a truth we just don't like. We try to divert our own attention away from both the startling external reality and the feelings provoked within us. Frequently this is a fear or a shame we have about our motivations and desires, and buried deep within out heart lays a truth we simply are frightened to admit.

Scripture tells us that Peter denied Christ out of fear. He was afraid that confessing his association with Christ would result in physical harm to himself. But instead of addressing his fears, or perhaps his desire for safety and security, he ignored or concealed them and therefore denied his association publicly, and took the easy way out.

Denial derails a man's rite of passage toward discovering the insecurities that lie within his heart. It may publicly make him appear strong in the moment, but on the inside he has taken a cowardly approach.

Rather, men who are called to act will recognize the impulse to deny, search deep for the reason they feel that way, and then embrace the insecurities they have. They address their insecurities headlong, including their fear and shame, and hold to truth, leaning on God's strength when they feel weak. In the end they hold to the truth and welcome all of its consequences.

Men who are called to act will recognize the impulse to deny, search deep for the reason they feel that way, and then embrace the insecurities they have and choose to act godly.

Self-Justification

On one occasion an expert in the law stood up to test Jesus. "Teacher," he asked, "what must I do to inherit eternal life?"
"What is written in the law?" He replied. "How do you read it?"
He answered: "'Love the Lord your God with all your heart and with all your soul and with all your strength and with all your mind" and

> *'Love your neighbor as yourself.'"*
> *"You have answered correctly," Jesus replied. "Do this and you will live."*
> *But he wanted to justify himself, so he asked Jesus, "And who is my neighbor?"* Luke 10:25–29

This is not a great moment for this religious lawyer. In debating the truth with Jesus, he hopes to make himself appear righteous, but ends up looking ridiculous.

Jesus craftily responds to the lawyer's question with a story, and the lawyer is forced to listen. Jesus of course does not directly answer the lawyer's initial question. Instead he lays a trap, a real conundrum that will force the lawyer to admit his own failings. Here's the story:

> *In reply Jesus said: "A man was going down from Jerusalem to Jericho, when he fell into the hands of robbers. They stripped him of his clothes, beat him and went away, leaving him half dead. A priest happened to be going down the same road, and when he saw the man, he passed by on the other side. So too, a Levite, when he came to the place and saw him, passed by on the other side. But a Samaritan, as he traveled, came where the man was; and when he saw him, he took pity on him. He want to him and bandaged his wounds, pouring on oil and wine. Then he put the man on his own donkey, brought him to an inn and took care of him. The next day he took out two silver coins and gave them to the innkeeper. 'Look after him,' he said, 'and when I return, I will reimburse you for any extra expense you may have.'*
> *"Which of these three do you think was a neighbor to the man who fell into the hands of robbers?"*
> *The expert in the law replied, "The one who had mercy on him."*
> *Jesus told him, "Go and do likewise."* Luke 10:30–37

The lawyer knew that Jesus had called his bluff, exposing his attempts to justify his unwillingness to help those who were not like him.

When we try to justify ourselves we listen only for the answers we want to hear. Rather than genuinely listening, we can listen only partially, since *our* truth is crowding out *the* truth. In addition, we hear counter responses as personal attacks since we have personalized our truth. As a result, we fail to learn how to own up to our errors in judgment and continue to live in a reality all our own. Self-justification obstructs growth on a man's journey toward manhood. It effectively stunts his growth.

God's man understands that there is only one who justifies, and that is God. When we self-justify, we trap ourselves by playing God, and thus the motivation and desires of our heart are only thinking of self. Even the way we ask questions reveals our real motivations, and false truths snag us in a snare of our own making. The only way forward is a growing self-awareness and transparency that counteracts the resistance of our heart.

Men who are called to act will listen by rejecting the voice of self-justification and by growing in self-awareness and transparency.

Blaming

> *The man said, "The woman you put here with me—she gave me some fruit from the tree, and I ate it."* Genesis 3:12

Blaming requires a real gut check because it's often our first response to sin. After the first sin, Adam notoriously blamed the woman for his own conscious decision to sin. But a closer look reveals that Adam was blaming not just woman, but God himself. Note his words, "*the woman you put here with me.*"

Ouch. Not man's finest moment.

When we cast blame, instead of hearing and responding to the whisper of God's truth and acknowledging our wrong desires, and thus wrong choices, we attempt to shift responsibility away from self to someone else. We blame others for our miscues and missteps.

Casting blame is a means of deflecting attention from the known desires that have led to our subsequent choices. Even though we are conscious of why we did it, we do everything to deflect attention away from our selfish motives. In Adam's case, he wanted to be *like God* and have knowledge of good and evil, something that was previously out of his reach.

Blame has no part in a man's rite into Christian manhood. The more we blame, the more calloused our motivations and heart become.

God's man, on the other hand, always softens his heart acknowledging his sin and the suffering it causes, becoming increasingly sensitive daily for his need to listen deeply to God.

Men who are called to act will listen by softening their hearts and rejecting the call of sin, stopping the progression of blame, and then becoming more sensitive to the truth of God.

Attacking

Now Abel kept flocks, and Cain worked the soil. In the course of time Cain brought some of the fruits of the soil as an offering to the Lord. And Abel also brought an offering—fat portions from some of the firstborn of his flock. The Lord looked with favor on Abel and his offering, but on Cain and his offering he did not look with favor. So Cain was very angry, and his face was downcast.
Then the Lord said to Cain, "Why are you angry? Why is your face downcast? If you do what is right, will you not be accepted? But if you do not do what is right, sin is crouching at your door; it desires to have you, but you must rule over it."
Now Cain said to his brother Abel, "Let's go out to the field." While they were in the field, Cain attacked his brother Abel and killed him.
Genesis 4:2-8

Sometimes when we are faced with an uncomfortable truth, we attempt to put the truth to death by means of human strength. Attacking may seem effective, but its short-lived gains are counterproductive in the long term. In Genesis 4 Cain's competitive and selfish desires for God's favor were unmediated, even after being warned by God, and therefore his feelings were personalized, swelling into anger and uncontrollable rage. Rather than celebrate Abel's accepted gift, which would have been the right response, he felt slighted and consciously devised a way for regaining his lost acceptance. Cain's action was to kill his brother–he tried to take the advantage he felt he lost.

While our attacks are rarely as substantial as Cain's attack, we will attack by accusing others, using aggressive language, and responding with anger in an effort to defend ourselves. We will direct our attacks toward the one who delivers the truth to us or toward other involved parties. In either case, what we are attempting to do here is to overpower truth with our preferred version of reality. *Attack* is the polar opposite of listening, because attack is listening to the self and preserving self by all human means possible.

When we move to attack others, we have lost the willingness to address the issues of our motivation. We have escalated our calloused desires to the point of taking offensive action against the party that has challenged us. This is not a Christian man's rite of passage. While movies sensationalize male vengeance and imply that attacks are our only means of justice, vengeance is never ours to take. Spiritual maturity demands that we do not attack people, but rather our determination to ensure that our *"desires will not have us, but we rule over them."* There is also a point where our attacks result in damage that cannot be undone. This could be as simple as an angry word spoken to our child, wife, parent, or friend. These attacks can result in wounded hearts that become permanently scarred. I can almost immediately recall certain painful words that were spoken to me; they have affected me for my entire life.

God's man is willing to listen carefully to his desires, considering the consequences of acting on them. God's man considers the future impact of his godly–or ungodly–words and actions. Every man will make occasional mistakes, but God's man is ever growing in wisdom and vision for the future, aligning his desires with God and being ruled by him.

Men who are called to act will listen by thinking through to their desires and the consequences of acting on them.

These four dysfunctional responses: *denying*, *justifying*, *blaming*, and *attacking* all represent a failure to effectively discern our motivations and desires, which in turn prevents us from effective listening. None of them represent the receptivity of God's man nor exemplify a rite of our passage into manhood. They are the marks of a man whose growth is stalled, stunted, and stubborn.

But the good news is that such a man can always change. And when he does finally listen at the deepest level, he will produce incredible growth.

Listening Effectively

Men must do serious spadework to listen. The soil of our hearts in many cases needs to be softened so that our motivations can be addressed. Jesus doesn't make any false promises here; he assures us that attentive hearing and deliberate action will be hard work. A true rite of passage is never easy; it's challenging. And it's challenging because competing voices are vying for our heart's attention. We all are stubborn in one area or another; each of us will find certain false messages to be compelling. Our task, then, is to seek truth at all costs and to listen with the right motive. If we can set aside our pride, Jesus promises a staggering payout—up to one hundred times our initial investment! This investment results in changed peer relationships. It results in committed, selfless marriages. It results in willingly respectful children. And it results in fulfilling careers. But remember: this is only a result of desires and motivations that have become completely aligned with God and his truth, which we *hear* and *act* upon repeatedly. For when a man's heart is aligned with God's will, the impact is felt in all parts of his life *and* by other people. Motivational change results in deep receptivity that is readily noticed and infectiously productive.

What's at stake here is nothing less than Christian manhood and the advancement of the gospel in and through your life.

So what are some steps we can take to listen more effectively? Here are four steps every man can take today to hear and act more effectively.

First: Accelerate

> *My dear brothers and sisters, take note of this: Everyone should be quick to listen, slow to speak and slow to become angry.* James 1:19

Any man can be *quick* to speak and *quick* to be angry. These are not accidental behaviors but learned behaviors—but so is *quick listening.* When we carelessly speak our mind and lose our temper we do so because these learned behaviors succeed in getting us what we want. The repeated success of these techniques results in a truncated listening process, and next time we almost instinctively select these tactics again. The same holds true for tactics rooted in quick listening. When we slow down our impulsive non-listening tendencies and discover the wisdom and insight of others, we'll find ourselves listening more quickly. As these insights lead us to experience success, we will no longer hesitate to listen well. So, if listening is the combination of *hearing* and *acting*, the goal of *quick* listening is met by closing the gap between our hearing and acting. But remember, we are applying this not only to listening to people, but most importantly to listening to God. When we listen to the truth and actively bring ourselves into alignment with that truth more quickly, it changes our desires over time. We thus allow less time for denial, justification, blame, and attack to surface and instead readily do what God requires. Great men do not protest as God confronts them with the truth; they obey without argument because they know that God's best is their best; they are quick to listen to him. These men have shortened the gap in their hearing and acting. They are accelerated listeners.

God's man listens effectively by acceleration: closing the gap between godly hearing and godly acting.

Two: Anticipate

> *In the morning, Lord, you hear my voice; in the morning I lay my requests before you and wait expectantly.* Psalm 5:3

I love those first three words "*in the morning.*" This is not a poetic inclusion by the psalmist; this is strategic and practical advice. Nothing helps our listening more than starting each day focused and in a position of listening. I know when I start my day this way my heart is tuned to listen throughout the day. While my devices, email, and social media cry for my attention, they hold nothing of significance for me. In fact, they may deafen my ears to the words of truth. But whenever I start the day with even a little scripture, prayer, and reflection, my heart becomes attentive to the things of God. Rather than moving through my day by my own strength and acting on my own truth, my attention is turned to anticipating God's strength based in his truth. And here's the thing: God's truth is available in rich quantities, but we are often not listening to it nor do we anticipate it. But the man who begins each day with God discovers that God speaks, and he speaks a lot. We need only pay attention to hear the voice of God through the circumstances of life.

God's man has an eagerness in his relationship with God, greeting each day with enthusiasm and excitement. He is expectant for answers because he has laid requests before God and lives in anticipation of how God's answer will take shape throughout the circumstances and events of the day. He is now tuned to listening not for his will, but God's will.

God's man listens effectively by eagerly seeking and anticipating a God who is always speaking.

Three: Accept

> *Whoever gives heed to instruction prospers, and blessed is the man who trusts in the Lord.* Proverbs 16:20

Life goes much better for men when we are willing to accept the truth. Not only should we accelerate our listening and anticipate God's response, but we also need to be quick to accept God's truth and act accordingly. Great and godly men *"heed instruction"* and *"trust in the Lord."* As Lord, God is the ultimate source of man's wisdom. Our response is merely trusting obedience, and since we believe God can be trusted, we should trust with great faith.

We do live in a world, however, where mankind cannot always be trusted. As a result, many men have a hard time trusting God. But these trust issues dissipate when we discover that God's truth works every time. With increased success we discover that God can be trusted, and we see what results from readied acceptance of his truth. Soon we will trust his truth even when we don't fully understand God's instruction. We will have become *quick* to listen!

God's man listens effectively by accepting, heeding, and trusting in the Lord and not the world.

A Final Thought

In the end, we can all be better listeners. All men need the life skill of listening. No one is exempt. We must give attention to others and work at get better at it. This is how we grow in our relationships with other people and with God.

There are some simple things we can do to begin the process. Here's a short list of tactics to help you get moving:

- *Demonstrate that you hear by looking a person in the eyes while they are talking.*
- *Remind yourself to give all your attention to the person talking.*
- *Practice K.M.S. (Keeping your Mouth Shut).*

- *Take notes as you hear, and repeat what you hear for clarity.*
- *Don't compose solutions when someone is talking.*
- *Ask clarifying questions when someone is done speaking.*
- *Accept responsibility for your issues, contributions, and needed corrections.*
- *Take action immediately to demonstrate you were hearing the other person.*

The more we give attention to how we hear and act, the more proficient we'll be as listeners. As we learn to do this more quickly in human relationships, we should also become more proficient in our relationship with God. After all, it's not just people we need to listen to; God is the one who provides truth. Later in the book we will learn how to more effectively hear from God himself. In the meantime, let's strive to improve our response time between hearing and acting.

3

The Hesitation of Men

"The only thing necessary for the triumph of evil is for good men to do nothing."

EDMUND BURKE

The Hesitation

Deep down, most Christian men have an insatiable urge for growth, development, and advancement–in short, to be better men. At a minimum we want to be seen as great men, husbands, fathers, and leaders. The only problem is that we don't know the path from where we are to where we want to go. Even without clear direction, we will still try to make progress.

We will try, try again, and then try some more. But after a while our list of failures becomes hard to ignore. Add even a little of bit of criticism and this feeling of failure will begin to consume our thoughts and adversely impact our perception of our identity. Rather than having moments of failure, we will begin to see ourselves as failures. Before too long we'll stall out and many throw in the towel.

These short moments of hesitation can become a type of ongoing paralysis, or apathy, which is fatal to the spiritual development and progression of men. But why do we hesitate? We are men empowered by God himself, so why do men get stuck in perpetual spiritual hesitation? The reasons are remarkably simple and straightforward, yet the specifics vary from man to man. Take Peter as an example.

Simon Peter was one of Jesus's first disciples and would become the leader of the church in Jerusalem. Jesus clearly saw his leadership potential, making him one of his three closest confidants. Jesus knew that Simon would become a key leader in the founding of the church; Jesus christened him *"Peter"* or *"Rock"* because he saw a strength in him unmatched by the others. In essence he was the Duane Johnson of the apostles (but maybe a little shorter and less physically developed).

Peter was without a doubt a leader who was called to act. He was a New Testament legacy leader who did a few things that no other man has done since. But he also had his moments of hesitation. The three hesitations he had in the last hours of Jesus's life are especially interesting. When things got heated, Peter froze, just like you or I might do. Peter, our gregarious, impulsive man of action, hesitated.

But why? Let's see what his hesitations can teach us about our own struggles.

Wrong Inaction

> *Then he returned to his disciples and found them sleeping. "Simon," he said to Peter. "Are you asleep? Couldn't you keep watch for one hour?"*
> Mark 14:37

Peter's first hesitation happens just moments before Jesus is arrested. It was fourth and goal; everything was on the line. But given simple instruction by Jesus to pray and keep watch, Peter drops the ball by taking a nap. Apathy at its finest. And I get it, he was tired. I have been there too. Peter and the other disciples were so tired that the posture of prayer was too much for their tired, aching bodies; the silence and darkness lulled them to sleep in no time.

Yet even in exhaustion a body will be alert when the moment demands it. We can be utterly and physically drained, yet the body will jolt to attention if we experience real stress and urgency. But Peter and the others did not feel such urgency. While the entire group fell asleep, it is Peter that Jesus admonishes; after all, Peter is supposed to be the spiritual *"Rock,"* not the man asleep like a rock. Please note there is nothing wrong with getting rest; Jesus well understood the need for sleep. Jesus is simply stunned that Peter still doesn't understand the urgency of the present moment. They're just seconds away from the grand finale.

Sometimes men hesitate because we don't sense any urgency; we don't see the need to be alert. We fail to see the predicament before us, and therefore we don't bother to ready our best game. When we allow other less relevant things to consume our physical energy, we become depleted of our spiritual attentiveness, resulting in failure in the very moments when we are most needed.

I cannot tell you how many times I have been in this situation as a man. I enter my home depleted and therefore perform poorly as a husband or father because I have used all my best spiritual energy at work. Or a business trip takes the wind from my sails and therefore I bring a bad attitude with me into other relationships, damaging my Christian witness. Or I get too focused on getting things done that I don't take time for divine interruptions that may give way to incredible opportunities. When we fail to manage our spiritual attentiveness or ensure that our spiritual awareness is high, we are in danger of succumbing to spiritual hesitation. Thus we experience failure, and it may also result in us feeling like a failure. All from wrong inaction.

We hesitate to do the godly thing by doing the human thing—which is to do nothing.

But this is only one of Peter's hesitations. Here is the next.

Wrong Action

> *The men seized Jesus and arrested him. Then one of those [Peter] standing near drew his sword and struck the servant of the high priest, cutting off his ear.* Mark 14:16–17

Peter's second hesitation occurs just moments after the previous incident. This time it's not a hesitation of *inaction*, but a hesitation to *determine the best action* and then act on it. As a mob approaches to arrest Jesus in the Garden, Peter, who is armed, reacts–or maybe he overcompensates for his last mistake. He reaches for his small, belted sword and swings it at a soldier named Malchus, severing his ear from his head. While he does not hesitate to act, his action is misguided. Within seconds, Jesus miraculously restores Malchus's ear, thus undoing the damage inflicted by Peter's wrong action.

As men, sometimes we hesitate to take the steps necessary to discover the right action. These failures stem from our inability to see God's larger vision. But of all men, Peter should have understood it. Jesus had explained his plans to Peter more than a few times during their journey to Jerusalem.

> *From that time on Jesus began to explain to his disciples that he must go to Jerusalem and suffer many things at the hands of the elders, the chief priests and the teachers of the law, and that he must be killed and on the third day be raised to life.* Matthew 16:21

We can see that Peter did not appreciate or understand Jesus's plan. In fact, he was strongly opposed:

> *Peter took him aside and began to rebuke him. "Never, Lord!" he said. "This shall never happen to you!"*
> *Jesus turned and said to Peter, "Get behind me, Satan! You are a stumbling block to me; you do not have in mind the concerns of God, but merely human concerns."* Matthew 16:22–23

Because Peter impulsively protested God's plan and vision, he hesitated to pursue the deeper meaning and submit to it. Therefore he acted, but unfortunately in a way that contradicted God's will–thus leading to wrong action. Many end up taking a wrong course of action because we don't understand and, in our ignorance, don't know how to join in. Our vision, plans, and ideas of how we believe things should be overshadow God's vision and even the ability to see doing life any differently.

We hesitate to do the right thing by doing our thing, which is the wrong thing.

But there is one more hesitation. Again, just moments later (Yep, not a good day in Peter's life.)

Lordship Issues

> *While Peter was below in the courtyard, one of the servant girls of the high priest came by. When she saw Peter warming himself, she looked closely at him. "You also were with that Nazarene, Jesus," she said. But he denied it.*
> *"I don't know or understand what you're talking about," he said, and went out into the entryway.*
> *When the servant girl saw him there, she again said to those standing around, "This fellow is one of them." Again, he denied it.*
> *After a little while, those standing near said to Peter, "Surely you are one of them, for you are a Galilean."*
> *He began to call down curses, and swore to them, "I don't know this man you're talking about."*
> *Immediately the rooster crowed the second time. Then Peter remembered the word Jesus had spoken to him: "Before the rooster crows twice you will disown me three times." And he broke down and wept.*
> Mark 14:66–72

Hours later, Peter's third hesitation relates to his association with Jesus. It is a fail of epic proportions. It goes down as the fail of all fails.

He hesitates to tell the truth about his association with Jesus, and all four Gospel authors—Matthew, Mark, Luke, and John—make sure to tell us about it. How would you like to have your fail recorded in the most purchased book of all time, and in all four accounts of Jesus's life?

Men hesitate, like Peter did here, primarily because we are afraid to let go. A helpless feeling creates a kind of fear that has men grasping for control. In Peter's case, out of an instinct of self-preservation, he hesitates to own up. We are sometimes too afraid to admit that we feel out of control. For a man loss of control seems less than masculine. Our desire to appear competent outweighs our desire to reveal our authentic selves. Therefore, we hesitate because we still want to do our thing—which again is the wrong thing.

Here's why: when we initially give our lives to Christ, we secretly want to hold on to some things. We don't say it, but it's how we feel and it's what we are thinking. Secretly we still have some things we want to do, boundaries we want to break, and motivations we'd rather not acknowledge. We retain a tight grip on friendships, vocation, finances, and the future; we simply are not ready to let go. The bottom line is this: we love Christ as a Savior but are cautious of Christ being our Lord.

We love the idea of salvation and the mutual idea of someone who saves. If the truth be told, when we are down and out, we want to be rescued from all our bad decisions. And the Bible teaches that we need a Savior to rescue us from our own bad intentions, decisions, and even the suffering that comes from these intentions and decisions. But here's the rub: It's hard for men to immediately and fully accept submitting to a Lord, one who is now the leader of our life. And Jesus is both: Savior and *Lord.*

The word *Lord* implies total life surrender to the leadership of another, in this case to the person of Jesus. Jesus was emphatic about our need to surrender to his lordship. We have a new life leader; we must leave our ways behind, take up his ways, and follow obediently. But this is hard for men, especially when we have spent so much of our lives learning to trust ourselves and avoiding reliance on others. When our sense of human self-sufficiency kicks in, obedience to the Lord challenges us to the core. This is what I mean when I say we love Christ as Savior, but we are hesitant and *cautious of Christ as Lord.*

We embrace Christ as Savior, but we are hesitant and cautious of Christ as Lord.

The lordship issue Peter faced in the courtyard is one every man faces. We may even encounter this come-to-Jesus moment thousands of times during a lifetime. In the face of lordship men hesitate, and lean on old processes, attitudes, beliefs, and actions. Being confronted with the lordship of Jesus Christ is a little unnerving. Like Peter did here, we, too, will hesitate on occasion. We succumb to feelings of fear and a concern for self-preservation.

But lordship requires us to relinquish control—and *each time* we encounter a moment of decision, we can either trust his lordship or hesitate. This is part of our daily spiritual exercise. We are always learning to give God another desire, submit another decision, and trust him for the outcome in another part of life. Instead of seeking to maintain control over our own lives, we must learn to entrust lordship to God. Over time, as God proves his faithfulness, we can learn to submit and obey more quickly. Thus we hesitate less.

At the core, these three hesitations in Peter's life reveal the primary reason we hesitate: we are consumed with self-interest and pride. We tend to be aware of a few of our selfish and prideful tendencies, but pride is more deeply ingrained and sinister than we realize. Peter hesitated and failed in each of these situations because of the deceptions of pride that affected his beliefs, attitudes, and actions on a level he was not prepared to address. These heated moments drew this pride out of him and exposed it for the world to see. While these moments of failure can be quite embarrassing, the man of God can face them with resilience, not further hesitation. It's just part of the process of becoming a man who is more fully surrendered day after day. Being confronted with our pride is a means of worship and sacrifice for the man of God. As a result, day after day, when confronted with our self-interest and pride we should not hesitate, but rather go all in so that the next decision is not about us but about Christ our Lord.

The Remedy: Go All In

> *Then Jesus said to his disciples, "Whoever wants to be my disciple must deny themselves and take up their cross and follow me. For whoever wants to save their life will lose it, but whoever loses their life for me will find it. What good will it be for someone to gain the whole world, yet forfeit their soul? Or what can anyone give in exchange for their soul?"* Matthew 16:24–26

Jesus understood that man is prone to hesitation. He knew we would hesitate even as young or old believers. And Jesus understood that pressing on through the hesitation would not be easy for us.

Jesus fully understood that addressing one's pride is not for the faint of heart; Jesus himself was no coward. Some people have an impression of him that is overly meek, soft, and lacking in masculine strength. But this is not true. Jesus was a courageous adventurer who chose a challenging way of life; he was a beacon that compelled others to follow him into the greatest adventure of their life. He taught that men would face enormous trials. Some of the challenges were external: fights, opposition, physical abuse, and ridicule. But even more, he knew that followers would encounter internal challenges that result in us wrestling with our desire for self-preservation. Because of this Jesus calls men to total commitment. Our path to becoming a man of God is one that renounces the path of least resistance. As followers, we deny our claim to certain privileges, endure trials that others avoid, and follow in the path of someone greater than self. Jesus dared men to go all in and not just dip their toes in the water.

It's a way of life with severe implications that require three choices.

Surrender to God's Interests

First, going all in requires a man to surrender to God's interests by *"denying self."* It begins with stopping this one thing: our claim to selfish privileges. Put simply, to *deny self* we need to say no to any word that begins with *self*: *self*-satisfaction, *self*-security, *self*-assurance, *self*-confidence, *self*-centeredness, and so on. We must deny self in every corner of our life and accept God in every corner of our life. Thus we are no longer in the lead; God is. Life no longer revolves around self, but rather him. The only way we can make sense of God's life is to actively, consciously, and daily deny self.

All in men deny themselves and accept God in every corner of their life.

Sacrifice to God's Way

Second, we must sacrifice living our way from now until our last breath. *"Taking up our cross"* is a vivid illustration of the sacrifice Jesus requires of godly men. Sacrifice in the Roman Empire was torture, not a cakewalk! When a man made a choice that resulted in Roman crucifixion, you would assume he was sold out to the values, beliefs, and actions that resulted in crucifixion, which was, and still is, the most painful form of execution known to man. When a man was sentenced to be crucified, one thing he was required to do was carry his own cross to the place of his public execution. Carrying his cross showed forced submission to the rule and power of the Roman government to the last breath of air–death by suffocation on a cross. If you thought denial of self is challenging, it is only the beginning; Jesus's all in lifestyle demands total sacrifice. It means a man must not only stop living for himself, but also live sacrificially each day until his last.

All in men bear up under the pain of daily sacrifice for Jesus.

Submission to God's Identity

Third, when Jesus said, *"Follow me,"* he intended for us to submit to his teaching. Following Jesus means we must subject ourselves to his teaching and to his identity. In Jesus's day, the words *"follow me"* were spoken by a teacher to a student and implied a change of the student's identity. This is the final requirement of the all in man. God's man is subject both to the teaching and the identity of the teachings of Jesus Christ. We now find our identity in Christ, not the self. We publicly acknowledge this change of identity by calling ourselves Christians, which means *"followers of Christ's teaching and way."* We pledge our allegiance to Jesus's service, on top of denying self and taking up our cross. Followers now have a whole new identity that is birthed from the teachings of Christ.

All in men pledge allegiance and priority to Jesus's teaching and follow his way.

Second Chances

While it's easy to pick apart the hesitations of Peter on his path to becoming the all in man, I'm glad we have records of each of them. Peter is just like any of us. He is an all in man, yet he suffers a few intermittent failures. Moments of hesitation led to these moments of failure. He was *not a failure*, but *a man who failed*–and discovered God's grace to keep moving forward. Peter's hesitations give us the opportunity to see that God still loves us in spite of our failures.

Peter was not a failure but a man who failed who needed God's grace to keep moving forward.

The well-known account of the *reinstatement of Peter* is a great source of hope for all men who hesitate. Our God is a God of second chances for all men, and this reinstatement of Peter is merely one biblical account of grace among many. It takes place on the lakeshore in Galilee just days after

Peter's three previous fails and after the resurrection of Jesus. Peter is back in his fishing boat and had been fishing all night without much success. Jesus, in one of his famed resurrection appearances, shows up on the shore, but the men do not recognize him. Jesus inquires to see if they have caught anything as of yet, and the men respond no. Then we hear Jesus say this:

> *"Throw your net on the right side of the boat and you will find some." When they did, they were unable to haul the net in because of the large number of fish.* John 21:6

Peter immediately recognizes that it has to be the resurrected Jesus; he leaps out of the boat and swims toward him. After breakfast, Jesus takes Peter aside. Note that this is the same Peter who couldn't stay awake in the garden, cut off Malchus' ear, and denied Jesus three times.

> *When they had finished eating, Jesus said to Simon Peter, "Simon son of John, do you truly love me more than these?"*
> *"Yes, Lord," he said, "You know that I love you."*
> *Jesus said, "Feed my lambs."*
> *Again Jesus said, "Simon son of John, do you truly love me?"*
> *He answered, "Yes, Lord, you know that I love you."*
> *Jesus said, "Take care of my sheep."*
> *The third time he said to him, "Simon son of John, do you love me?"*
> *Peter was hurt because Jesus asked him the third time, "Do you love me?" He said, "Lord, you know all things; you know that I love you."*
> *Jesus said, "Feed my sheep."* John 21:15–17

This reinstatement is powerful. It illustrates a number of things, but most of all it reveals that God never gives up on men.

Jesus wants us to trust him more through each failure, and he wants us to hesitate less each time. He continues to love us and pursue us with infinite grace, forgiveness, mercy, and love. While we may believe God will no longer use us, and so ashamedly go right back to doing what we were doing before (fishing or whatever) he implores us to stay the course. It's through hesitation and failure that we learn to trust God a little more next time, thus giving him lordship over another unseen area of our life.

The voice of self-disqualification is no match for God. He wants us to charge ahead, staying true to his mission, living life without regret. And the best part is: he wants to dust us off and help us move from the bench back to the game, just as he did with Peter.

Men Who Did Not Hesitate

There are also some great men in the Bible who *did not hesitate*, and we can learn even more from them. The following men did indeed have some moments of failure, but their lack of hesitation in *hearing* and *acting* teaches us a lot about what it means to be a man of God.

Here are five such men.

Abraham | Non-Hesitant Obedience

> *Some time later God tested Abraham. He said to him, "Abraham!"*
> *"Here I am," he replied.*
> *Then God said, "Take your son, your only son, whom you love—Isaac—and to the region of Moriah. Sacrifice him there as a burnt offering on a mountain I will show you."*
> *Early the next morning Abraham got up and loaded his donkey. He took with him two of his servants and his son Isaac. When he had cut enough wood for the burnt offering, he set out for the place God had told him about. On the third day Abraham looked up and saw the place in the distance. He said to the servants, "Stay here with the donkey while I and the boy go over there. We will worship and then we will come back to you." Abraham took the wood for the burnt offering and placed it on his son Isaac, and he himself carried the fire and the knife.*
> *As the two of them went on together, Isaac spoke up and said to his father Abraham, "Father?"*
> *"Yes my son?" Abraham replied.*

"The fire and the wood are here," Isaac said, "but where is the lamb for the burnt offering?"
Abraham answered, "God himself will provide the lamb for the burnt offering, my son." And the two of them went on together.
Genesis 22:1–8

Abraham was pretty quick to obey. We don't see debating, questioning, or even a need for clarification. This is hyper-unusual for any man, mainly because we want to understand everything in its entirety before taking that first step of obedience. Not Abraham. He did not hesitate. He is numbered among the greatest men of God of all time because he understood that God was his primary provider, not himself.

Again, Abraham was not perfect, but he was all in with God and did not hesitate in this greatest of tests. As we know, God provided a ram for the sacrifice in place of Abraham's son, but it was provided at God's time, in God's way, and at the place of God's choosing. A couple of millennia in the future God would provide another sacrifice–the sacrifice of Jesus–on this same mountain and in the same location. What a testimony to this all in man! A father, man, husband, and leader that was willing to obey without compromise, even when the stakes were high. He is an example for all men. The lesson is this: live a life of non-hesitant obedience and simply do what God asks.

God's man never hesitates to obey.

Noah | Non-Hesitant Righteousness

God saw how corrupt the earth had become, for all the people on earth had corrupted their ways. So God said to Noah, "I am going to put an end to all people, for the earth is filled with violence because of them. I am surely going to destroy both them and the earth. So make yourself an ark of cypress wood." Genesis 6:12–13

While this flood was devastating for mankind, we should fix our attention on Noah and his family. Here was a righteous man. He stood out from all the rest of mankind and faithfully led his family toward righteousness in a corrupt and evil society. Have you ever felt like you are in a similar position?

Noah did not conform to society, nor did he fall to social pressure; he remained a resolute, all in man who worshipped God alone and walked in righteousness. He did not hesitate even when God asked him to build a boat in the middle of the desert prior to it ever raining a day on planet Earth. Talk about an enduring, non-hesitant man! He obeyed no matter how ridiculous his behavior seemed to an unfaithful world. Noah is again an example for all men. The lesson is this: live out non-hesitant righteousness, even amid public pressure and personal loneliness.

God's man never hesitates to be righteous in an unrighteous world.

David | Non-Hesitant Reverence

David asked the men standing near him, "What will be done for the man who kills this Philistine and removes this disgrace from Israel? Who is this uncircumcised Philistine that he should defy the armies of the living God?" 1 Samuel 17:26

David never hesitated to believe that God could defeat Goliath even though everyone else hesitated to act. This man was a stand-alone example of extreme reverence of God in the face of an entire army that hesitated to take action. Thus, David's story continues to be told today.

I cannot read this story without being moved by David's audacious reverence of God. He is willing to risk it all on a stage that features two armies, two nations. Surely everyone in the Israelite army is holding their breath as David runs out to meet this giant. If he loses, the loss will be catastrophic. But David understands that this is not a war between him and a giant man; it's a war between God and an irreverent man and pagan nation. God wins this battle because one young man does not hesitate to revere the Lord. The lesson is this: live in non-hesitant reverence and watch God win every battle.

God's man never hesitates to revere God.

Daniel | Non-Hesitant Character

> *Now when Daniel learned that the decree had been published, he went home to his upstairs room where the windows opened toward Jerusalem. Three times a day he got down on his knees and prayed, giving thanks to his God, just as he had done before. Then these men went as a group and found Daniel praying and asking God for help. So they went to the king and spoke to him about his royal decree: "Did you not publish a decree that during the next thirty days anyone who prays to any god or human being except to you, Your Majesty, would be thrown into the lion's den?"* Daniel 6:10–12

Daniel never wavered as he worked for multiple, unbelieving kings. In this instance, God miraculously saved him, just as he had preserved the lives of Daniel's friends in a similar situation. Daniel did not hesitate to do what was right and to honor his Lord. When Daniel was challenged, he never failed to live in godly character. No wavering. No hesitation. Character and resolve describe this man of God. The lesson is this: live out non-hesitant character regardless of the challenges before you.

God's man never hesitates to act in godly character.

Peter | Non-Hesitant Faith

> *Shortly before dawn Jesus went out to them, walking on the lake. When the disciples saw him walking on the lake, they were terrified.*
> *"It's a ghost," they said, and cried out in fear.*
> *But Jesus immediately said to them: "Take courage! It is I. Don't be afraid."*
> *"Lord, if it's you," Peter replied, "tell me to come to you on the water."*
> *"Come," he said. Then Peter got down out of the boat, walked on the water and came toward Jesus.* Matthew 14:25–29

I saved this one for last because Peter has many redeeming qualities. At this moment Peter became the only fully human man to ever walk on water. This could only happen because he did not hesitate to act in faith. While we can pick apart his hesitations and failures, we have to hand it to this guy. Here he did something no man had ever done and may never do again. He walked on water. Actually, I am a little jealous. Good job, Peter, for not hesitating. The lesson is this: live out non-hesitant faith by just getting out of your metaphorical boat.

God's man never hesitates to take a step of faith.

Hesitation in our faith is a common challenge among men, but it does not need to be. God is looking for a man who does not hesitate but courageously and boldly follows him. The five men above were prototypes of the man called to act. Aspire to be like these men in your *obedience*, *righteousness*, *reverence*, *character*, and *faith*, then watch as God establishes nations, saves people, wins battles, builds character, and fortifies faith through these acts of obedience. Remember: Christ calls, empowers, and restores all men. He desires that we become all in, Lord-submitted, non-hesitant men of God.

Are you with me?

4

The Essentials of Listening

Learning to Hear

So faith comes from hearing, and hearing through the word of Christ.

ROMANS 10:17

It's no surprise, but the way men hear is far different from how women hear.

I know, shocking.

In the book *Gender and the Brain*, Leah Ariniello has discovered that the male brain is on average 10 percent larger than female brains. But don't get all bigheaded, men, for she has also discovered that female brains contain far more brain cells. That's interesting for sure. And this study, along with other current research, has taught us something we probably already intuitively knew— men and women hear differently. (If you've been married for five minutes, you know this!) Overall men tend to hear facts and opinions, take conversations at face value, work out solutions for problems before the other person is finished talking, and demonstrate far less emotion in their connection and responses. Women, on the other hand, hear every tiny piece of data, connect emotionally, and frequently overanalyze the communication exchange. And we quickly learn that we both have something to work on in order to hear more effectively. We can and will improve our hearing if we acknowledge our tendencies and build skills in the needed areas of weakness—or at least learn to manage those weaknesses. For example, we men might listen more fully by simply tuning in emotionally and resisting the urge to offer a solution right away.

But as Paul the apostle states above, *"Faith comes from hearing."* This is because hearing is an absolute essential to faith. God makes available to us all the information we need, but if we do not successfully hear it, we will never know how we are to become men that are called to act.

Therefore, fellas, we must learn to hear.

Components of Listening

At the most basic level, hearing is just the awareness of sound. What we're after is intentional hearing that incites response. Perhaps a more accurate word here is *listening*. To listen, we need only do a few things well. Listening is merely hearing with purpose. As men who are called to act, we must first discern how to act. Which means we must learn how to *listen* to instructions.

There are three components to effective listening: *attention*, *receptivity*, and *action*.

Attention

"Whoever has ears, let them hear." Matthew 11:15

God looks forward to speaking with us. You may be surprised by this, but he is excited to speak to all mankind. God has always been communicating. He communicated from the dawn of time and will until the end of time. He communicated directly to early fathers, kings, and prophets. And as we turn toward the New Testament, we discover that Jesus was God's ultimate messenger. Jesus is called *"the Word of God made flesh."* God sent Jesus primarily to communicate to us, to tell us about heaven, grace, and how he enabled restoration in our relationship with God. Jesus made it clear that if we've got *ears*, we need to *hear* —he wants us to listen!

But to listen, we need to give our full attention.

For example, if I am going to listen to my boss, wife, or child, I need to give my full attention to them by being fully present with them when they are in the room and talking with me. I must eliminate all other distractions and instead focus in, for when I do, I demonstrate that the person speaking is important and that what they want to discuss is also important. The same is true of God. Listening demands that I give God my attention and am fully present with him; the things he says are important; therefore, I should attentively tune in.

> *Now the Berean Jews were of more noble character than those in Thessalonica, for they received the message with great eagerness and examined the Scriptures every day to see if what Paul said was true.*
> Acts 17:11

The Bereans understood this. They listened to Paul, but even more, they wanted to hear the truth from Paul. This meant they not only listened attentively, but they went as far as fact-checking everything against scripture, doing so *"with great eagerness."* Now that is giving superior attention! So to listen we must first give our eager attention, especially if we believe that God wants the very best for us.

Receptivity

> *So, as the Holy Spirit says: "Today, if you hear his voice, do not harden your hearts as you did in the rebellion, during the time of testing in the wilderness." Hebrews 3:7–8*

Receptivity is the inward evidence of our outward ability to listen to others. It's the posture of a willingness and openness to hear.

Men often learn to be more receptive when we are placed in situations where we recognize the limits of our own self-sufficiency. Such was the case of the Hebrews that wandered around in the wilderness. It took 40 years of testing for their hearts to soften. In the desert, they were driven toward complete dependence on God–and increased receptivity.

But there is evidence like this all over the Scripture. For example, the apostle Paul became receptive when struck with blindness (Acts 9). The Philippian jailer was far more receptive when his life was at risk for losing the prisoners under his care (Acts 16). Peter was more willing to be fully committed to the work of Christ after his threefold denial and threefold confrontation by Jesus (John 21).

But the best evidence is the evidence from our own lives. For men, it's failure, (or decreased self-sufficiency) that drives us toward increased receptivity. For some men failure is the only teacher. We wish this were not the case, because it is so reactive rather that proactive. But for men it's pain, failure, and low self-sufficiency that teaches us best. It teaches us both the limits of self (a needed lesson) and also the need for truth outside of the self. When we experience pain, we want to remove it by any means possible, therefore we become receptive to anything that will address the pain. The higher the pain, the higher the receptivity, which is why for many men their first experiences with Christ and brotherhood involve ministries that directly meet the need and heal the pain. Cases in point are divorce groups, chemical addiction groups, financial support networks, prison ministries, and so on.

It's interesting that it takes so much work to be receptive. This is because receptivity is *active*, not a passive activity. And as men called to act, we sometimes think that action is only something we visibly do, but this is not the case. Sometimes the struggle with apathy is a private and personal battle, unseen by the world. In this case, being receptive means that we battle against a private and personal monologue that happens within our mind. It's battling against an inner monologue of immediate critique when receiving feedback. It's battling against an inner monologue of judgment when hearing another person's ideas. It's battling against an inner monologue that attempts to fix the issue before a person is done talking. It's *actively ceasing* the inner monologue altogether and putting our mind and heart in a place of openness, rather than shutting others down or out. But it requires some hard work to remove these internal and external distractions. That's receptivity.

But remember, we are talking about receptivity to God. I think this is why God let the Hebrews wander for so long in the desert. He wanted men to become receptive, but their hearts were *hard.* And for some it will take years—hopefully not 40—to become more receptive to God. A place where the voice of self lays down its biases, presumptions, bad beliefs, and former worldviews. A place where God speaks and we listen—and we hear with softened hearts.

Action

> *Do not merely listen to the word, and so deceive yourselves. Do what it says.* James 1:22

The determining factor of our listening is not only *attention* and *receptivity*, but also our subsequent *action.* To hear the truth and not act is to choose to live in deception. It's to be self-deceived. Action is required. The challenge is that we don't always obey the first time we hear something, which means that now we must not only act, but also acknowledge our previous choice to live in self-deception. This is not easy for men to do.

There is a New Testament word that describes religious people who live in conscious self-deception—hypocrite. A hypocrite is a stage actor; he is someone who pretends to do the right thing. He acts like he is doing the right thing, yet does it from the wrong motivation—to merely put on a show. Hypocrisy can include pretending to act, acting from the wrong motivation, or teaching righteousness while acting in unrighteousness. Jesus frequently comes on strong against all forms of Christian hypocrisy because it both lacks integrity and it is a poor witness of God's character. God hates hypocrisy because it contradicts his nature and because it results in Christian misrepresentation to an already confused world, a world that needs to *listen,* but is *hearing* the wrong message from the behaviors and motivations of our lives.

And these three components are necessary for effective listening. You see, it's not just hearing–it's listening, which involves giving *attention*, becoming *receptive*, and moving to right *action* for the right reason. And when we do this with God, our faith is spurred and our relationship is strengthened.

It's not just hearing–it's listening, which involves giving attention, becoming receptive, and moving to right action for the right reason.

The Noise that Affects Our Hearing

He replied, "Blessed rather are those who hear the word of God and obey it." Luke 11:28

One of the primary ways we hear God is through scripture. We will get into this in far more detail in chapter 8, but scripture contains the *words of God* for men called to act. We must focus on listening to God through the reading of scripture, which turns our attention, receptivity, and action toward things that matter. But listening to God in scripture is no ordinary task; it's reading with purpose, seeking to understand what God wants from us and for us in life.

Unfortunately, there is a lot of noise that gets in the way of a man's ability to listen to God. But once in a while there are men who overcome these noises. Either they don't hear the noise, they hear it and ignore it, or they hear the noise and have a counter response. Young David, who became King David, was one of these men. And his story, his best story, is one full of noises that he overcame.

So back when David was just a youngster, he had learned to listen to God. When David met Goliath, he was only a young teen. He was the youngest of eight brothers–all sons of a man named Jesse. Three of David's brothers were off at war while David (as the youngest) was home taking care of his father's sheep. One day, Jesse, concerned about the three sons at war, sent David with some supplies and food and told him to find out how his brothers were doing.

We all know the end of the story–David slays Goliath–but it's the lead-up to the confrontation that has a lot to teach men about the noises we encounter. There were eight noises that David had to ignore in order to act as he did. So listen up, and discover the genius of David in these eight moments.

Fear

> *Whenever the Israelites saw the man, they all fled from him in great fear.* 1 Samuel 17:24

This is a laughable moment. The Israelites are fortunate that no video footage exists, because the sight must have been humiliating. For 40 days they came out to the battle line. For 40 days they gave battle cries. And for 40 days, whenever *"the man"* Goliath marched out, the warriors of Israel scattered and ran.

Fear is debilitating in a man's life and often embarrassing. We fear being seen as foolish, which causes many of us to refuse to take a stand. We fear making a decision that will cost us something. While we portray masculine confidence on the outside, inside we often struggle with private fears. And it's fear that kept the Israelite army from moving against Goliath, yet David was able to overcome the noise of this fear.

Fame

> *Now the Israelites had been saying, "Do you see how this man keeps coming out? He comes out to defy Israel. The king will give great wealth to the man who kills him. He will also give him his daughter in marriage and will exempt his family from taxes in Israel."* 1 Samuel 17:25

The allure of fame most of the time is a real problem for men. It's an ongoing temptation and its appeal is strong. Yet in this situation, the offer of fame could not persuade an already paralyzed army. The promise of fame spoke to the men's selfish desires, but it turned out they valued their own life still a little more. King Saul's cunning proposition resulted in a silence that was deafening to an entire army of men.

Attractive as King Saul thought that fame would be, it's still the wrong motivation for a man of action. Men who hear and act should act on principles based on truth, not in pursuit of fame or approval. Although David acted, he was not motivated by Saul's offer of fame. Rather, David desired to silence Goliath's insult to the God of Israel. David acted for the right reasons, with proper motivation; disinterested in the fame this moment would produce.

Disgrace

> *David asked the men standing near him, "What will be done for the man who kills this Philistine and removes this disgrace from Israel? Who is this uncircumcised Philistine that he should defy the armies of the living God?"* 1 Samuel 17:27

Disgrace is like an incessant static hiss within the heart of a man.

Most men have experienced some form of deep and even public disgrace. Some men spend much of their life in concern that someone new will discover what happened because it was so damning and embarrassing. This disgrace and shame can prevent men from hearing and acting when they know what they should do. The noise of disgrace prevents any forward movement.

David was shocked to find that no man would step forward to accept Goliath's challenge and defend God's honor. Maybe this was because of their imminent concern about potential disgrace. David turned the tables on the noise of disgrace by declaring that defeat on the battlefield would be a far lesser disgrace than hesitating to do their duty. Again he overcomes the noise of disgrace and with it his countrymen's cowardly inaction.

Ridicule

> *When Eliab, David's oldest brother, heard him speaking with the men, he burned with anger at him and asked, "Why have you come down here? And with whom did you leave those few sheep in the wilderness? I know how conceited you are and how wicked your heart is; you came down only to watch the battle."* 1 Samuel 17:28

Every man has been ridiculed or slandered. That ridicule can come from those close to us, as David received from his brothers. In spite of our godly confidence, the opinions and potential ridicule of others can keep us from acting when we know we should. Ridicule and gossip can hurt, yet David was not about to let this noise derail him from God's mission. Again he laughs in the face of this noise and dismisses the ridicule of his brothers.

Insufficient Preparation

> *Saul replied, "You are not able to go out against this Philistine and fight him; you are only a young man, and he has been a warrior from his youth."* 1 Samuel 17:33

When we become aware of our deficiencies, how often do we say to ourselves, *"I am not qualified to do that"*? And sometimes that assessment may well be true. It was certainly true here for David. How, after all, could a mere teenager go up against the hero of the Philistine army? What David understood was that God was calling him to do something, and it was that conviction that drove him to act. Not his age. Not even his stature. Not his preparation.

No one is ever fully prepared, but we always have enough. Every man called by God is indwelled by the Holy Spirit; and whenever a man of God blocks out the noise and listens to God, this Spirit makes up for every human insufficiency, which means God's man is called to act, and qualified to act.

Human Ingenuity

> *Then Saul dressed David in his own tunic. He put a coat of armor on him and a bronze helmet on his head. David fastened on his sword over the tunic and tried walking around, because he was not used to them. "I cannot go in these," he said to Saul, "because I am not used to them." So he took them off.* 1 Samuel 17:38–39

Some men by nature want to think their way out of difficult situations. And I have known many men who are indeed extremely intelligent—seemingly well equipped to solve their own problems. But given our vast abilities, we can outsmart ourselves and be lured into self-reliance and a false sense of security. Over time we might even persuade ourselves to listen more to our own ingenuity than to God.

David was not about to play it safe. He was simply going to do what God was calling him to do with the tools he had already been trained with. David didn't need weaponry or armor, nor any other kind of fortification that human ingenuity could provide. Besides, these tools were custom built for an adult king, not a young shepherd boy. So David cast off this noise and was simply obedient to the voice of God; using a few shepherd tools, he ran out to meet his opposition. And while victory seemed improbable, human ingenuity is just noise to the man of God. The sword God intended David to use was in the hand of his enemy; David would slay Goliath with the giant's own sword.

Intimidation

> *He looked David over and saw that he was little more than a boy, glowing with health and handsome, and he despised him. He said to David, "Am I a dog, that you come at me with sticks?" And the Philistine cursed David by his gods. "Come here," he said, "and I'll give your flesh to the birds and the wild animals!"* 1 Samuel 17:42–44

When we do not get our way, we often resort to trash talk to intimidate others into doing what pleases us. And when we are the recipients of the trash talk, we will at times reluctantly surrender our position. We are all too aware of the personal, financial, and social power of others–or even their physical stature, as in this case. Intimidation can keep us from acting, speaking out, or confronting perpetrators of injustice because we feel small and weak in comparison.

But David was undeterred. He ignored the noise of the intimidation of this giant and even reinterpreted it through the wisdom of God. We, too, must be deaf to this noise.

Procrastination

> *As the Philistine moved closer to attack him, David ran quickly toward the battle line to meet him.* 1 Samuel 17:48

I love that David runs with utter abandonment. He runs headlong, burning the bridges of return behind him. There is no turning back; he will face his opponent.

Many men wait too long, and therefore live in the static of procrastination. We hear a little voice that says we will do this or that *"when I retire," "maybe later,"* or *"when I have enough money."* This is exactly why we men are not running, as David did here. Had David not overcome the noise of procrastination, we would not have this record of the greatest mano-a-mano battle in all of history. We would not have this shining example of a man answering the call to act.

Men who listen are able and willing to cut through all the noise and cut to the chase. They are aware of the noise around them, but they do not dwell on it or let it hijack God's voice. They hear the voice of God with clarity, moving the noise around them to the background till it becomes distant and irrelevant. They are men who hear well and act well.

So be *attentive*, *receptive*, and *act* listening to the right voice.

5

The Five Voices All Men Hear

Listening to The Right Voice

Most of us know that being a man requires tremendous strength and courage. But it also requires a keen ear so that we know where to focus that strength and courage. Understanding this is crucial to our growth and development as a man, leader, and—if not now, perhaps one day—husband and father.

In fact, we must not only effectively listen by giving attention, increasing receptivity, and taking right action; we must not only avoid the noises of fear, fame, disgrace, ridicule, insufficient preparation, human ingenuity, intimidation, and procrastination; we must also listen to the right voice.

It took me years to understand this. What I'm about to share with you took me years to discover, but if you listen carefully to what you are about to read, it could aid you all your life and change how you listen.

Aside from the challenges we face above, there are *five voices* shouting at men. These five voices are heard frequently each day. Given the day's particular circumstances, certain voices will be louder than others. But these voices have incredible power to direct our life. They have the ability to direct or misdirect our thoughts, attitudes, and actions, leading us toward either life and godliness or loss and destruction. The key for us, then, is to become aware of the voices when they emerge, to identify them, and even to redirect them. If you can do all that, you will experience greater success in this life.

Voice One | The Man that We Think We Are

> *They replied, "Let one of us sit at your right and the other at your left in your glory."* Mark 10:37

Every man wants to be legendary; therefore, *"the voice of the man we think we are"* is sometimes the loudest voice. Men want to hold a trophy, stand on the platform, and be praised by fans on a global stage. Perhaps you know someone who is a legend in his own mind? On some days, this will describe you. But it is dangerous for men to listen to this self-aggrandizing voice. It's evidence of our deepest arrogance, and if we don't address it, our fall is imminent.

This is pride, and its voice comes in many forms, ultimately planting a thought in our mind that impacts our beliefs, attitudes, and actions. And what is that corrupting thought? That we are better than we are in reality. What we say and do as a result of this belief is rather selfish and makes us look self-centered. I wonder if James and John were under the influence of this kind of voice when they made the statement in the verse above. In positioning for the most honored status in Jesus's kingdom, they only managed to win that day's *"Most Clueless"* award (which apparently was a fierce ongoing competition among his disciples).

I'm sure you have bumped into a few arrogant guys in life. Men who are masters at their skill, talent, or gift–and have allowed their mastery to master them. These men are destined for a great fall; so don't make their mistake. Avoid certain demise by tuning out this voice of arrogance.

Voice Two | The Man Others Think We Are

But the Pharisees and the teachers of the law muttered, "This man welcomes sinners and eats with them." Luke 15:2

Yes, it's true: others have a wonderful plan for your life. If you haven't discovered this yet, you soon will. Bosses, coaches, teachers, friends, and sometimes even your family project a manner of thinking about you. They reinforce their voices with tweets, snaps, posts, and opinions. Although they may not have malicious intent, their propaganda reflects the man *"they think"* you are. This is merely their perspective. Their view seems right to them, whether you like it or not.

But you don't have to conform your life to what they believe. Again, it is only the man *others think* you are. The truth is, when family, friends, and colleagues tell us what they think about us, we tend to find these voices to be compelling, their sound bites insightful. In moments of emotional vulnerability, we can be persuaded to adopt their unique perspective. But we have to be careful. We need to remember that we are not the sum of what others think about us—even though this voice is persuasive. Genuine statements and genuine perspectives can be genuinely wrong. They can lead you down a path of destruction. While sometimes they are correct, more often they are wrong—or only partially correct.

As your identity is forming, the voice of influential friends, family, coaches, and teachers will be exceedingly loud to you. You might end up believing that everything they say—in particular what they say about you—is true. Take caution, however, because this leads to you living according to what *others expect of you*, which could be off-course and out of alignment with God's truth.

Many a man has chased after this voice, running from one opinion to the next. These men end up confused and exhausted. Even Jesus ignored these voices, seeing their potential to lead him down ungodly paths. Note the sound bite above from the religious leaders. Don't follow these ungodly voices or blindly believe what they say about you as the only truth.

Voice Three | The Man We Think Others Think We Are

> *"We seemed like grasshoppers in our own eyes, and we looked the same to them."* Numbers 13:33

This voice may appear a little confusing when you first hear it, but stay with me for a minute or two.

This voice is the one we hear when we lie down at night, staring at the ceiling. It speaks to us as we reflect on the happenings of the day, considering that occasional failure. It's the voice of our mind talking to our soul about what others think of us. This voice has incredible power because it develops thoughts about ourselves that, when combined with emotions, construct systems of belief about who we are.

The voice of *what we think others think* is a deceptive voice because it is powerful, private, and personal. Ultimately, it can take us down the wrong path.

Throughout my life, I cannot tell you how many nights I laid awake consumed with thoughts about myself and wondering what *others thought about me.* These voices disturbed me, echoing in my mind from across the timeline of my life. In bed, I heard the voice of an unloving father, an unappreciative wife, an unsatisfied boss, an unsupportive coach, and an unsupportive friend. Too often we allow these judgmental voices to persuade us of our lack of worth. We replay the sounds of these tapes, privately shaming ourselves, ruminating only on failure, and allowing these voices to control our lives.

Voice Four | The Man We Actually Are

> *For I know that good itself does not dwell in me, that is, in my sinful nature. For I have the desire to do what is good, but I cannot carry it out.* Romans 7:18

At some point, you are going to encounter the most challenging voice of all—the voice of your sin.

Yes, we men inflict harm, sometimes even intentionally, causing the people around us to suffer. You are already aware of this. But occasionally, the full depravity of your sin will announce itself to you. You will feel sin's full weight as you realize that you haven't merely made a mistake or hurt someone else; no, you committed an offense against God. Some days this voice will feel absolutely devastating. It will bring you to your knees, and you will see no way out—the voice of the sinful man, the *man you actually are.*

When this happens, I want you to remember you are not the first to feel this way. The apostle Paul, for one, was not shy in describing these moments of devastating clarity. Note his words above.

Now, while I want to advise you to ignore this voice, the problem is that this voice is telling you the truth. You sinned. You screwed things up. You made mistakes. You have indeed offended God and will again in the future. But that's not the end of the story!

This voice, as awful as it is, does help us by motivating us to look for a solution to our despair. This search leads us to a better voice, the last voice—the one you need to hear.

Voice Five | The Man God Says We Are

> *And a voice from heaven said, "This is my Son, whom I love; with him I am well pleased."* Matthew 3:17

In the end, there is only one voice that you should listen to, and only one you should hear and act upon. One voice to heed. One voice that is true. It's the voice of God. It's *the man God says we are.*

What God says—particularly what he says about you—is the only truth you should believe. The other sounds we hear are nothing but gibberish, sound bites from a world that is lost and confused. God's voice is the only true and reliable voice. God's voice is the only one that matters. It's God's voice that spoke you into existence. It's God's voice that echoes across time. It's God's voice that extends grace, love, mercy, and forgiveness to you when you hear voices that insist that you don't deserve it.

Men are daily challenged to hear the Father's voice. Yet God has said so many wonderful things about our relationship with him. Here are some of the things that God says about you:

You are a saint; you have been blessed in the heavenly realms with every spiritual blessing in Christ; you have been chosen; you have been adopted by God; you have redemption; you have been forgiven; you have his grace; you have been marked by the seal of the Holy Spirit; you have an amazing hope; you have power through the Spirit. (This is a small, partial list of what God says about you from Ephesians 1.)

Never underestimate God's voice. His voice is true. And never fail to listen to this voice when you hear him speak.

Throughout each day we will hear all five of these voices. We will listen to some more than others. And regardless of our age or stage in life, these five voices are loud. Even now, one of these voices is louder than all the others. The key is listening only to the right voice–the fifth one. Staying tuned to the man God says we are and then ignoring all the others. This is not the power of positive thinking; it is rather us becoming the man we already are. It's living in the redemptive power of God and seeing ourselves the way God sees us by listening only to his voice. It's living out God's identity, God's way.

The Voice of a Father's Affirmation

Men, it's your Father's voice that matter the most. It's his voice that utters the most beautiful sentence you will ever hear:

"This is my son [insert your name], with whom I am well pleased."

Of the three times we hear God's voice in the New Testament, twice God make this public proclamation to Jesus. The first time was at his baptism, and the second was on the Mount of Transfiguration. I think God says this primarily to Jesus so that he might hear the voice of affirmation of his father. But I also think God says this out loud so we might hear it, too. Because we ourselves long to hear this voice of affirmation!

All men long to hear the voice of God, but we must stop listening to all the other voices. We must shun them. We need to turn a deaf ear to them. And then we need only listen to the voice of God and the Father who created us.

If you mean to follow God, then follow only him. If you mean to become God's man, then listen only to the Father of all mankind. His voice is trustworthy, confident, dependable, and true.

In closing, note this last word from the Father. While Jesus was gathered with a few men on the Mount of Transfiguration, something significant happened. The same voice that spoke at Jesus's baptism was heard again. It was God who spoke. His words were mostly identical, but take note of the small yet meaningful addition at the end:

> *While he was still speaking, a bright cloud covered them, and a voice from the cloud said, "This is my Son, whom I love; with him I am well pleased. Listen to him!"* Matthew 17:5

6

A Man that Acts Fights Apathy

What words would you use to describe the present culture?

For me, the first word that comes to mind is *consuming*. Our culture has become seriously over-stimulated by media, entertainment, politics, pop issues, the overall speed of modern life–and the list goes on. All the things we consume that we thought would make life easier have not made life easier.

There is another word that comes to my mind–*shame*. Shame presents a real challenge for manhood. Both public and private shame now consume the mind of most men, which is making it more challenging to know how to act like a man.

Recent American culture has made it almost shameful to be a man. It appears we can no longer proudly wear our pronouns–he, his, him–without making some form of public apology for being born this way. With embarrassment, young men write them on their nametags as instructed by their educators; it often feels like a test of their *"pride."* This may be because we are told that men are responsible for most of society's ills: rape, gang violence, murder, mass shootings, oppression of the weak, violent crime, and even the endorsement and empowerment of men who do the same. And if this is not enough, vocal female counterparts have strongly opposed males as a gender in recent years, marketing messages against the male gender in hope of exposing ills and inequality, but at the same time leveraging that negative messaging to their advantage. In spite of all this I believe it is still good to be a man, to live unashamed, and be exceedingly proud to be a man. But how are we to do this? How can we be men and respond to these cultural challenges and shifts with love and grace and not forfeit everything that makes us a man? These are hard questions to answer, and even harder to put into action. But there *is* an answer.

This shame issue can become even more complicated if we are *male* and also a *Christian*; it can feel like the culture is pressing even harder against those of us in both categories. We feel we have to remain silent as the *"male oppressor and perpetrator"* and also silent about our beliefs for fear of *"proliferating or proselytizing"* others. Men everywhere (regardless of age) feel restrained by social pressure in our workplaces, in our schools, and on social media accounts. We fear being attacked and then publicly shamed.

As strange as it may sound, we have even become fearful of having these discussions in our churches, where we should be able to safely explore beliefs, have civil discussions about Christian character, and look deeply at the truth in God's Word without fear of being judged. This is the place where we should feel most free to pursue answers to life's questions. And men: we should not be ashamed of our faith. We should give each other opportunities to build the necessary fortitude for a faith that is strong, vibrant, and immovable. I believe this, too, is still possible, and that there is a way to do this that helps us on the path of becoming God's men and great men. But discovering how to do it is a serious challenge.

Our world has become overly sensitive to individual worldviews and individual rights and feelings, and this has had unintended consequences on social interpretations of masculinity and even on Christian manhood. One being *shame*. And we have not even touched on the private shame men experience.

The point is this: amidst all the public and private shame men experience, we are finding it harder and harder to know how to act. The power, authority, voice, and morality once handed to us by God seems to be slipping through our fingers. Men hesitate because of it, unsure of how to respond, and other louder or more robust voices take the opportunity to speak up and act out in hopes of gaining a following. In our hesitation, shame, and apathy, other agendas appear to be winning the day and the attention, hearts, and feelings of the masses.

So what is a man to do?

Men Need Action

The bottom line is this: the times demand that God's man needs to take more action, not less, action taken in the right way and initiated by right desire.

But many men feel boxed in by this pursuit. They feel trapped by culture; instead of freely exploring our manliness, we restrict ourselves to what our culture approves.

Here are three expressions of masculinity that are still acceptable in our time. Let's see what they teach us about the desires of men.

Sports & Entertainment - Strength

Men need ways to let out built-up aggression; we cannot just neuter men, so this aggression must be moderated. Men want to cheer on physical play in a sporting event. Men want to battle against friends in online gaming. And men may want to watch a violent movie or two, again and again and again. And while there are naysayers out there who condemn these outlets, we need safe outlets for exploring, understanding, and guiding our aggression. Nothing good comes about for a man with pent-up aggression that he doesn't know what to do with. And counseling can help, but it might be better to just go chop down a tree, hunt an animal, or compete in a game.

Men need safe outlets within culture, but it seems there are becoming fewer and fewer socially acceptable outlets for the testosterone we naturally produce. Without an available outlet, the chemical rush manifests itself through passionate thoughts, outbursts of anger, verbal aggression, competitiveness, domineering behavior, and even physical violence.

Several field studies have proven that testosterone levels increase during aggressive periods of sports play. This is why men act out like they do at times in football, baseball, soccer, and the like. While some people abhor the occasional over-aggressiveness, extra-curricular shoving match, or unsportsmanlike celebrations–honestly, are we surprised? These are just men, or rather very young men, learning how to moderate everything pent up inside within acceptable boundaries. They are trained, coached, and positioned to be aggressive, and then we highlight it and publicly eviscerate them after they cross an arbitrary, unacceptable line. Could this be a form of public shaming that further produces hesitancy in men? Or is it appropriate and necessary to keep them in line?

Men increasingly choose endurance conditioning as their preferred outlet, exhausting their bodies in the hopes of finding an acceptable release. Other men fulfill their need to compete through hunting, fishing, hiking, or climbing; we think of them as adrenaline junkies, but what if they are just looking for a safe outlet for their masculine needs?

Whatever form these outlets may take, all men need them. We need safe places to explore and even learn to moderate our innate physicality. We cannot ignore the chemical production of testosterone in our bodies that demands a physical release. But we need to ask ourselves whether we are using this chemical reality as a way to hide from a spiritual reality. We should not use a physical release, like a momentary act of aggression, to conceal the selfish and wild desires within our heart. For when we lash out physically, verbally, or emotionally at others, this may be a hint that something is out of balance within our heart. And it must be addressed.

Aggressive behavior is stirred by masculine insecurities. Whenever we lack strength, competency, or control in a given moment, we readily sense it. When we experience insecurity, we may feel weak. And feeling weak is emasculating for men who believe they must be strong, competent, and in control to be liked in life and loved by women. Therefore, what do we do? Well, we act out in aggression. We ignore the insecurity we feel and go right after the weakness by trying to regain strength by force.

Here is how the apostle Paul describes the outbursts of the insecure man:

The acts of the flesh [the insecure man] are obvious: sexual immorality, impurity and debauchery; idolatry and witchcraft; hatred, discord, jealousy, fits of rage, selfish ambition, dissensions, factions and envy; drunkenness, orgies, and the like. I warn you, as I did before, that those who live like this will not inherit the kingdom of God.
Galatians 5:19–21

Since many men have never learned how to address insecurities, they tend toward the list of aggressions above. And we men know many of these well. Some we know too well, acting out physically rather than acting out spiritually. And remember, we need to act out, but we need to focus our aggression on the right thing in the right way.

Men need to act out, but we need to focus our aggression on the right thing in the right way.

Unfortunately, we don't know how to do this. But Christ's strength can override our human insecurities, and he gives us good outlets, safe ones, for all our aggression, which Paul also taught us about.

I can do all this through him who gives me strength. Philippians 4:13

Finally, be strong in the Lord and in his mighty power. Ephesians 6:10

But he said to me, "My grace is sufficient for you, for my power is made perfect in weakness." Therefore I will boast all the more gladly about my weaknesses, so that Christ's power may rest on me. 2 Corinthians 12:9

Work & Career - Purpose

This comes as no surprise, but men use work and the pursuit of a career as an outlet for their masculine pursuit. Wives know it. Kids know it. Business executives know it and even leverage it. And managers accept it and reward it, thankful for the increased productivity.

There are many men who go to work to escape from the challenges at home. This is not an admirable mindset, and I do believe there is a deeper problem at play: men struggle when confronted with purposelessness and don't know how to find the strength of purpose they seek. Challenges at home expose our greatest feeling of weakness and our mutual quest for masculine strength. Men may escape to work environments where they feel stronger because we don't know how to pursue purpose at home, leadership at home, connection at home, and discipleship at home. At work we feel some semblance of control, power, and authority; here a command structure is clear, and we generally understand what is expected of us. Therefore we get lost in emails, phone calls, and work-related issues at every waking minute because every small win feeds our need for accomplishment. Yet the bigger sense of accomplishment that comes from living a life of purpose goes unmet. We, in a sense, use work to buy time, inoculating ourselves with purpose that immediately fades upon a layoff, job change, or retirement. I cannot tell you how many times I have met men from literally all over the world who say, *"When I retire, I plan on doing [fill in the blank with a noble-sounding pursuit]."* Among the Christian men I speak with, the most frequent word that fills in the blank here is *"ministry,"* which seems to me a clear lament of missing purpose.

Men want to feel purposeful. We want to discover and find our purpose in all aspects of life, but we seek it first vocationally because it seems to be a safe and easy pursuit. But this only meets some of our needs, not our real needs, and leaves so much lacking in our search for purpose.

Men want to discover and find their purpose in all aspects of life.

Consider these words from God found in the book of Jeremiah. In context, this is a letter that the prophet Jeremiah sent from Jerusalem to men who had been carried off into captivity to Babylon.

> *For I know the plans I have for you, declares the Lord, plans for welfare and not for evil, to give you a future and a hope.* Jeremiah 29:11

The good news is God knows when we feel a lack of purpose, and he declares there is a plan, a future, and hope for all men, individually and corporately, even during significant tribulation, when we feel all purpose is lost. In the middle of our confusion, we will be overwhelmed and lose ourselves in things that bring us some sense of accomplishment–but our purpose rests not in the things we do, but in the purpose God gives and who we are in Christ.

Men who become too narrowly focused on their present status will stay trapped in a meaningless pursuit. They will fail to see the bigger picture, our macro purpose, and how God's purpose connects to man's purpose.

Notice here how God is clear with Jeremiah at the beginning of the exile of the nation to Babylon.

> *The word of the Lord came to me, saying, "Before I formed you in the womb I knew you, before you were born I set you apart; I appointed you as a prophet to the nations."*
> *"Alas, Sovereign Lord," I said, "I do not know how to speak; I am too young."*
> *But the Lord said to me, "Do not say, 'I am too young.' You must go to everyone I send you to and say whatever I command you. Do not be afraid of them, for I am with you and will rescue you," declares the Lord.* Jeremiah 1:5–8

God knew that men would question themselves given the challenges before them, but he had a purpose for Jeremiah and every other man who lived during this time. Whether we are talking about the Babylonian captivity or your job at work, God is nevertheless giving us an opportunity to discover more of his purpose and your vocational purpose. Work does not have to be a means to an end. It can be a means to something greater, but only if we take the time to see God's purpose in it. It should drive us to acknowledge the grand purpose God has for us, which influences not only our work, but also our family, friendships, and neighborhoods. In seeing this we discover that God's purpose is greater, and enables us accomplish far more than just our work-related tasks. Men who discover this become men of purposeful action.

Men want to live a life of purposeful action.

Compulsions & Overindulgence - Relationship

Finally, we must address compulsions and overindulgence. Overindulgence of any kind is a common route many men take to explore their masculine longing. Faced with excessive materialism and consumerism, are we surprised that men overdo just about everything? Eating. Entertainment. Social Media. Drinking. Pornography. Our society welcomes us to consume without restraint.

Compulsions arise from our inability to understand how to satisfy our own desires, but they are also coupled with our abundant access to a wide variety of tempting material. To make matters worse, we might even find that friends, colleagues, and family members find our compulsions acceptable and encourage us to indulge them. This reinforcement from our community becomes a vote of affirmation. I know many men for whom drinking is their primary relational connection; they actually cannot imagine getting together with other people without drinking. Combined with relational acceptance it is what keeps us coming back for more. Therefore, giving up our compulsion and overindulgences would mean giving up the relationships that go with them. In the end, compulsion has become a method of escape not only from a vice-related hunger, but also from the empty feeling of loneliness. These activities may be the only context within which a man pursues masculine relationships.

Compulsion and overindulgence is not a new problem. But note the real issue: men have long been starving for relationship, companionship, and life-long friendship. And while we might be afraid to admit it, men tend to have very few good friends, so we don't dare risk losing the few we do have. Note this first record of a man in need of companionship.

> *But for Adam no suitable helper was found. So the Lord God caused the man to fall into a deep sleep; and while he was sleeping, he took one of the man's ribs and then closed up the place with flesh. Then the Lord God made a woman from the rib he had taken out of the man, and he brought her to the man.* Genesis 2:20–22

Just one chapter later man has an interesting response to his desire for relationship and companionship. Instead of stepping in to interrupt his wife's disobedience, he joins her in sinning. Could this compulsion and indulgence to eat have resulted from his need for companionship and acceptance? For sure, this was about getting something neither of them yet had, but in the end they wanted it *together*. To be clear, this sin was not some misguided, well-intentioned, self-sacrificial act of loyalty to each other, for as soon as God started handing out consequences, Adam's shame turns to blame.

> *[Adam] answered [God], "I heard you in the garden, and I was afraid because I was naked; so I hid."*
> *And [God] said, "Who told you that you were naked? Have you eaten from the tree that I commanded you not to eat from?"*
> *[Adam] said, "The woman you put here with me—she gave me some fruit from the tree, and I ate it."* Genesis 3:10-12

As men we desire relationship more than we care to admit. While occasional acts of machismo may suggest that we are strong, aggressive, and independent, our core need for acceptance and companionship is what truly guides us. We are willing to hang on to bad relationships and the indulgences and compulsions that go with them because we are ashamed to admit we don't know how to fulfill our desires in other ways nor how to stand up for what is right. Ultimately, we are afraid to risk the relationship at hand. This is true in many roles for men: as a husband, father, leader, and in relationships with friends. Our desperate need for relationship gives way to overindulgences and compulsions that continue over time in our attempt to escape the challenges we feel.

Men want companionship, but often there are vices that accompany some companions.

In my travels across the world, I've seen most men resort to these same three outlets; sports, work, and indulgences drive a man to explore their strength, purpose, and relationship. Men entrenched in American culture are no different than men in Asia, South America, or the Middle East. The same issues afflict men in First and Third World countries alike. Men are thirsting for action, looking for outlets that satisfy our deep longings unique to our gender. In the end we are just trying to find our way as men.

Male Atrophy

Our issues are complex, more complex than we, or others, care to admit.

While acceptable outlets for masculine pursuits appear to be disappearing, the bigger issue is that the process of becoming of a man is changing within our culture. The system by which we pass on manhood to the next generation is at risk. While manhood feels like it's under attack, we may be discovering that what is really under attack is God's design and his intended means of successful transmission for future generations. The transmission of God-honoring manhood is essential so that future generations of men know what it means to be a man. Shamefully, we have lost our way.

If we were to study our cultural landscape carefully, we would discover that fatherlessness is perhaps one of the great epidemics affecting us today. It impacts everyone. Fatherlessness, and I mean the absence of a male presence in the home, has serious negative impacts on marriage, children, and transmission of manhood. If addressed, it could perhaps help to cure a lot of the world's ills.

In a document released from the U.S. Department of Justice entitled, *"What Can the Federal Government Do to Decrease Crime and Revitalize Communities?"* we discover some startling statistics about the desperate need for male leadership in the home. And please keep in mind this is a secular study on the topic of crime and revitalization. It states that fatherless homes account for:

- *90 percent of all homeless and runaway youths,*
- *85 percent of all children that exhibit behavioral disorders,*
- *75 percent of adolescent patients in substance abuse centers,*
- *75 percent of rapists motivated by displaced anger,*
- *71 percent of all high school dropouts,*
- *70 percent of juveniles in state-operated institutions, and*
- *63 percent of youth suicides.*

Now that says something about the need for the father and how absence of a father impacts society on a whole. On the flip side, when a father is present in a home, there is an almost equal positive impact. Educational achievement goes way up, drug use goes way down, and incarceration rates go way down. This is all affected by one thing: a father who is present. Now consider the impact felt by a fully engaged father who also provides spiritual leadership. Think about the power and authority we possess that will be lost without the successful transmission of biblical principles to the next generation. I believe men can change the world. And while men are under attack, we cannot fail to transmit what God has given to us to the next generation. We cannot be apathetic.

Our greatest opportunity for exploration of manhood and male development is found right in the home. Male leadership within the family unit, combined with godly instruction, is the means of transmitting manliness.

> *Hear, O Israel: The Lord our God, the Lord is one. Love the Lord your God with all your heart and with all your soul and with all your strength. These commandments that I give you today are to be on your hearts. Impress them on your children. Talk about them when you sit*

> *at home and when you walk along the road, when you lie down and when you get up. Tie them as symbols on your hands and bind them on your foreheads. Write them on the doorframes of your houses and on your gates.* Deuteronomy 6:4-9

It was always God's plan for men to lead. First, they must *be led* by God and learn to love the authority of God with all their *heart*, *soul*, and *strength*. Then from this we are commanded–non-optional–to *impress*, *talk*, *tie*, and *write* as we *sit*, *walk*, *lie*, and *get up*. This is active, full engagement of the father in spiritual leadership and direction of the home from a submissive heart.

Now, for those of us who grew up in homes without a father, like myself, we know what we missed, and we at times feel years behind. For those of us who grew up in Christian homes or maybe experienced some of what this was like, as I did with my grandfather, we understand the significant spiritual value and impact. And for those of us who are first-generation Christian fathers, we get it, too. We understand that having a Christian male role model in the home makes a huge difference. But when we haven't been taught to be a man, husband, leader, and father, we'll have a lot of questions along the way, and we are often ashamed to admit it.

Our issues flow from what has–or has not–been transmitted to us. We cannot become godly men without having another godly man show us the way. Therefore what is really under attack, and always has been, is the transmission of God's message to all mankind. The only thing that will break this cycle is one man who chooses to actively pass this on to the next. But the resultant question is: what do we do when we have not been taught?

What do we do when we haven't been taught how deal with aggressions that arise from insecurity, how to address lack of purpose in our vocations and personal life, or how to curtail overindulgences that feed on relationships. If you ask a man if he understands how to deal with these issues, he will likely admit he doesn't know what to do. We lack the guidance needed to understand these issues, and we haven't been told what to do. In the end, I believe men escape to sport, work, and compulsions because we don't have any better ideas.

Take a moment and try to answer the following questions:

- *What is the best way to deal with my pent-up aggressions?*
- *What is the correct way to find meaningful purpose?*
- *What is the right way to build lasting friendships when I feel isolated and alone?*

Have you ever had a father discuss these questions with you? Have you ever discussed them with any other man? When's the last time this has come up in your men's small group?

Most of the time we are ashamed to admit we have these questions. Or maybe we are even more ashamed to only now discover the depth of our confusion. And because we are not discussing our issues, we are missing huge opportunities to discuss God-honoring manhood with men in a way that can help future generations of men.

And then male-pattern atrophy sets in.

Atrophy is the steady decline in the effectiveness of a muscle due to underuse. For those of us who have broken an arm or leg and worn a cast, we know atrophy. When we have to wear a cast or brace for an extended period, the atrophy can be severe. Muscle underuse causes the tissue and cells to deteriorate and break down.

And I believe *spiritual atrophy* among men is on the rise.

When I talk to pastors, men's leaders, and directors of men's ministries, they all concur that men are by far the hardest audience to reach. Some commiserate on this topic ad nauseum and live in frustration with men who are spiritually stalled, hesitant, and apathetic. Let's call it spiritual atrophy: a spiritual breakdown caused by male-pattern apathy. We must address this. While we can blame our family upbringing, liberal women's movements, the speed of society, the church, or the general pervasiveness of sin, at some point we have to stop blaming others and end the shame. We already tried shame and blame in the Garden, and God still called men to action. We must take responsibility for our *spiritual apathy* that results in *spiritual atrophy* by taking one step of godly action. It can all be changed with one man who acts.

Apathy is the worst possible option for men. When our motives are pure, action is always a good choice, even if it turns out we have picked the wrong action. We can learn from our actions even when we do the wrong thing. Wrong action is still movement and the use of spiritual muscles. Even if we do everything wrong, we will have learned another way not to do something in the future. But inaction discontinues spiritual development. Therefore the strategic place to begin the fight is with our enemy: apathy. Because *apathy* leads to *atrophy.*

The strategic place to begin the fight is with our enemy: apathy. Because apathy leads to atrophy.

A Man Who Fought with Apathy and Won

For a moment let's circle back to a story we have already referenced. The Old Testament battle between David and Goliath is perhaps the most famous battle in the Bible. Whether you know the story completely or not, let's dig into the narrative. David, a teenager, comes face to face with a nine-foot-tall giant warrior who has joined with the Philistines in battle.

But the fight was really a fight with male-pattern apathy and spiritual atrophy.

Imagine the location. It is a field in the Valley of Elah. Two enemy armies have encamped for war on opposite hills looking toward the valley between—the Israelites on one side and the Philistines, the God haters, on the other. The Israelites come to battle under the leadership of King Saul. King Saul has recently been appointed by the people as their nation's first king. He was primarily chosen for his size and stature; he stands head and shoulders above everyone else.

They have gathered for war, but for 40 days there has been no war. Only preparations made. Battle lines drawn. Daily cheers and chants against the opposition—but no war. According to custom, the commander shall either send the full army into battle or select a single man as the designated champion to challenge the other army's best fighter. In other words, each champion fights the battle on behalf of his army. The winner will take the other's plunder.

Each day, Goliath shows up on his hill and challenges someone to come and do battle *mano a mano*. Each day the same thing happens, and yet no one in the Israelite army has been willing to face him. The soldiers lack courage, will, and drive. They are apathetic, stalled, hesitant men in a downward spiral of confidence that appears irreversible.

But a young boy named David has come, and it's he who will teach God's people, the enemy nation, and all future men how to fight not a giant, but apathy. This is the battle all men must fight.

So how do we move from apathy to action? Here are six things that David did.

Take A Risk

> *David said to Saul, "Let no one lose heart on account of this Philistine; your servant will go and fight him."* 1 Samuel 17:32

Apathy's grip is strong for men. But to become a man of action, we have to be willing to fight against our own voice of inaction. Shame must not hold you back. Circumstances must not hold you back. Uncertainty must not hold you back. You must choose not to let apathy rule over you. As David arrived on the scene, an entire nation of men stood in apathy, physically and spiritually. Yet the boy who brought the meat and cheese platter to the field of battle is the one who will take the first risk.

As men, we must move from the bench to the game. We need to take some risk. To risk losing an old carnal relationship and risk building a new spiritual one. To risk engaging with Christian community. To risk standing up for our faith. To risk putting our heart out there. To risk sharing a challenge or fear. We begin the battle by taking a small risk and then repeating it regularly.

Fight apathy by taking small risks daily.

Acknowledge Preparation

> *"Your servant has been keeping his father's sheep. When a lion or a bear came and carried off a sheep from the flock, I went after it, struck it and rescued the sheep from its mouth. When it turned on me, I seized it by its hair, struck it and killed it. Your servant has killed both the lion and the bear; this uncircumcised Philistine will be like one of them, because he has defied the armies of the living God. The Lord who rescued me from the paw of the lion and the paw of the bear will rescue me from the hand of this Philistine."* 1 Samuel 17:34–37

God is always preparing his man. He has been doing this since the beginning of time. And he was preparing David from a very young age. David's job shepherding sheep was apparently a belittling task in the eyes of everybody else, yet he knew that God was preparing him for something big. Here in meaningless activity, God was giving him meaning. God was preparing David for a life of fighting apathy. These small battles were not about shepherding or hunting but were setting the stage for a life of fighting the spiritual battle against apathy.

God has gifted all men and wants them to advance the kingdom. Regardless of your line of work–plumber, carpenter, electrician, financial advisor, accountant, salesperson, lawyer, or executive–God has called you to act and thus influence this world. What's interesting is that, just like David, God has been preparing you since you were young for action in his kingdom. He wants you to recognize that preparation; you are called to act and speak on behalf of God in whatever way you are able. While you might think this preparation is insignificant and somewhat unspiritual, how spiritual is slinging a stone? It matters not what you do, only that you do it and recognize that it is God, not man, preparing you. In fact, God has already prepared you with skills, talents, and resources that others do not have. It's not merely a sling and a stone; it's a sling and a stone in the hand of a man prepared by God.

Fight apathy by realizing you are a man prepared by God.

Halt Human Reason

> *David fastened on his sword over the tunic and tried walking around, because he was not used to them. "I cannot go in these," he said to Saul, "because I am not used to them." So he took them off. Then he took his staff in his hand, chose five smooth stones from the stream, put them in the pouch of his shepherd's bag and, with his sling in his hand, approached the Philistine.* 1 Samuel 17:39–40

What is especially intriguing about this moment is that King Saul is the natural choice to fight the giant, given his own impressive height. Yet he gives David all his custom-made, oversized gear and weaponry. Talk about a head scratcher. Talk about a contrast. This moment is laughable if you take a moment to consider its preposterous nature.

In an army full of apathetic men, King Saul is the most egregious offender. King Saul is the man who should have walked out into battle and fought Goliath, but instead apathy set in and glued him to the bench, out of the game. Saul essentially and symbolically hands the entire kingdom over to a boy. In this episode God shows King Saul and the nation of Israel that David–the one not shackled in apathy–is his next choice for king.

I love the moment when David puts the armor on. He tries to walk around in it, which is a well-meaning and rational gesture of goodwill to his king, though absurd. Please remember, this is not to be a human vs. human battle. David quickly understands that the gesture is kind but the logic is wrong, and he throws the gift and the logic to the side. When you see him go out to the battle, he will utilize the tools with which God has already equipped him. David's strategy is to activate faith against human reason, not fight by human strength.

Men lean too much on human reasoning, strategy, and logic, which is exactly why we don't act. We don't act because we'd rather figure it all out on our own, develop a fail-safe strategy, and know the end before we ever begin. This is exactly what holds us back or causes wrong action. Not that human reason is bad, it just has limits. At some point we have to admit that we've reached the end of human logic and act in faith.

If anyone has ever told you that what you were doing was crazy, then you know what it means to reach the end of logic. Men should reach for more of these moments: in marriage, family, work, church, neighborhoods, and beyond. When we push the limits of human logic while staying grounded in biblical truth, we may look back and see that our small act had miraculous results, and it's in these moments men are made. We may discover that we are living more expectantly and come to the realization that maybe what we have is already enough.

Fight apathy by remembering that where human logic ends, God begins.

Speak God's Will

David said to the Philistine, "You come against me with sword and spear and javelin, but I come against you in the name of the Lord Almighty, the God of the armies of Israel, whom you have defied. This day the Lord will deliver you into my hands, and I'll strike you down and cut off your head. This very day I will give the carcasses of the Philistine army to the birds and the wild animals, and the whole world will know that there is a God in Israel. All those gathered here will know that it is not by sword or spear that the Lord saves; for the battle is the Lord's, and he will give all of you into our hands."
1 Samuel 17:45–47

If we could play this moment back in high definition and slow motion, I wonder if we would laugh or shiver. Imagine a teenage boy shaking his staff at a 9-foot-tall warrior and his shield bearer while voicing this judgment on him. It's a chilling prophecy that will be fulfilled to the letter in mere seconds. And what's startling about this is how David is so confidently focused on God. David is consumed with thoughts of God. He understands this is not a battle between boy and giant—this battle is between a swearing, insulting, God-hating man and the Almighty God. And in the end, it is God who will defeat Goliath. It is God who will defeat the Philistines because they have brought disgrace to the Mighty One. Human reality has faded for David, and all he sees is a spiritual reality, and therefore as he acts—and notice this—he *speaks* God's will, not his own.

We would be much better served in marriage, parenting, work, and life if we only spoke God's will and not our own. When the heat is on, if we spoke less from our mind, our judgment, our desires, and our will and instead drew only from God's heart, just consider how much better life would be. If we could see the issues we face with spiritual vision, and in light of spiritual battles, how much more we would fight not our own battles, but the battles God wants us to fight. But this means we must be less apathetic to the spiritual tone of every moment and recognize what God wants us to do, rather than what we want to do. Being less apathetic means our will takes a back seat to God's will, which we speak regardless of how we feel.

Fight apathy by speaking God's will, not your own.

Charge

> *As the Philistine moved closer to attack him, David ran quickly toward the battle line to meet him.* 1 Samuel 17:48

Notice what David does here: he *runs*. As soon as David steps onto the field of the battle, he knows that there is no turning back. He has burned the ships, the bridges, and the road to return. This is not a walk. This is not a stroll. This is a run, and David is set to engage in an all-out and all in sprint and battle to the finish. It's inspiring. I wonder what this looked like in high-definition slow motion. One day God will play this back for us all in heaven, and we will stand in amazement.

To act, you are going to have to charge at the issue—your issues. At some point, when you're battling the tendency of apathy in your life, you've got run into it. You've got to run into it with abandon. You've got to run into it as if you've forgotten about everything else. Go ahead, leave it all behind. You need to go all in; push in all the chips. There's no turning back.

There is something that activates in a man's life when he goes all in. For when a man goes all in, something incredible happens. This is where the great stories begin. Stories of victory, accomplishment, beginnings, and fulfillment. I think men are too easily convinced to merely dip their toes in the water, but this is not enough. No one is inspired by a man who dips his toes in the water, but when a man goes all in, it inspires us all. When a spiritual man charges, then God-sized miracles happen. Are you missing a miracle in your life? Try charging into all in action.

Fight apathy by charging with abandonment into godly action.

Finish

> *Reaching into his bag and taking out a stone, he slung it and struck the Philistine on the forehead. The stone sank into his forehead, and he fell face down on the ground. So David triumphed over the Philistine with a sling and a stone; without a sword in his hand he struck down the Philistine and killed him. David ran and stood over him. He took hold of the Philistine's sword and drew it from the sheath. After he killed him, he cut off his head with the sword.* 1 Samuel 17:49–51

When we retell this story, we often choose to sanitize these gory and beautiful details. Yet it's the best part! David sent a stone at this man with his sling, which struck him dead between the eyes. Remember: David is not fighting this physical battle. David's fight is against apathy; God is the one battling Goliath. Keep in mind, there are thousands of men standing around watching this moment unfold, standing deep in the pool of apathy. They have had forty days to prepare for this fight. While the giant Goliath was demanding a challenger, none of these men responded. They were apathetic. They had done nothing and said nothing in the face of injustice and sin. Yet a young man now came onto the scene, and he was willing. And while they saw the boy David fighting, the one actually fighting was God. It was he who carried this stone and sunk it into this blasphemous man, causing Goliath to fall forward and bow before God and the nation of Israel.

But then the gory part: David walks over to this guy and lops off his head. Not with David's nonexistent sword, not with Saul's bigger-than-average sword, but with Goliath's unreasonably large sword. He yanks it from Goliath's side, pulls it from its sheath, and proceeds to remove his unusually large head from his body. Then David carries this man's head and sword back from the battle. Now that's an ending I want God to play back for me in heaven, but I would love it if he panned to the two armies–I assume there were a few seconds there that everyone was in shock. I'll bet David's brothers and King Saul had to pick their jaws up off the ground.

There is a great lesson here. In all this gore we see that sometimes when we act against the impulse of apathy, we discover the resources we need, not back in the tent, but out in the field of battle. God is preparing resources out there that he wants us to go and get, which we can only do by the activation of our faith against spiritual apathy. The sword God wanted to give David was in the battle; David had to go get it, and God knew he would.

Fight apathy by believing God will provide the victory you desire, but remember the resource you need may located in the battle. So fight to the finish.

Don't Do Nothing

Apathy is *doing nothing* and *saying nothing* when God has called us to *act* and *speak up*.

Do something; don't do nothing. When a man acts, he learns. Whether he acts rightly or messes up, an attempt at faithful obedience is where we need to start. These experiences will help us learn just what to do or what not to do in the future.

You will fail on occasion, but this does not mean you are a failure. You've only discovered another way to not do something, which is better than doing nothing. So stop doing nothing. Doing nothing is exactly how we got into the problem of sin in the first place.

In the Garden, man did nothing and said nothing.

Instead be a man, God's man, one who acts.

PART TWO

The Activities of a Man Who Acts

7

Five Fundamentals

Vince Lombardi, widely considered the greatest coach in football history, would begin each season's training camp the same way: "Gentlemen," he said, holding a pigskin in his right hand, "this is a football." Lombardi understood the power of re-teaching and relearning the fundamentals of blocking, tackling, and formations every season. Although the players thought those elementary things were trivial, they learned to respect Lombardi, and the team went on to win five NFL championships in seven years. We can achieve the same success in our spiritual journey when we stick to the fundamentals laid out in God's Word.

Like many of you, I struggled with the fundamentals early in my Christian journey, and to some degree, I still struggle. We often want to move on from these disciplines, thinking they're too trivial. Can't we just focus on the *"deeper issues"* of the faith (whatever that may mean)? But I have come to discover that Coach Lombardi was right. We need to know the fundamentals and practice them. And we need to know them well because we will be forced to address them time and time again. They are foundational to every aspect of our Christian walk.

The Overview of the Fundamentals

I have found that the following five disciplines are critical for men. These disciplines are the fundamentals in our faith development. They teach us how best to run, pass, catch, block, and tackle in our faith (so to speak). Each of these fundamental activities is necessary for both *hearing* and *acting*. They are how we *listen*. They aid in us progressively becoming more like Christ, in becoming *the man God wants us to be.*

They are not built on human ingenuity; they are timeless tools that Jesus used with his men. Disciples have since passed these on from generation to generation. They are the means of our growth regardless of our physical age or spiritual stage. They are made for the novice and the mature alike, for young and for old. They are just as relevant to us today as they were to men living 2,000 years ago.

These fundamentals are not the means of our salvation, but rather a means of growth that comes out of our salvation. This is an important distinction; it is only Christ who saves. Only Christ saves men from sin that separates us from God. Our salvation is complete in his work by means of his life, death, and resurrection.

These fundamentals are not the means of our salvation, but rather a means of growth that comes out of our salvation.

These fundamentals are not vehicles of God's grace (something God does). They are not attributes of virtue or character (something we aspire to be). They are not the outcomes we seek (the produce of our action). Very simply put, these activities are things we do to develop God's kingdom. These activities are simply tools every man should leverage regularly throughout his lifetime. They resolve how a man is trained to hear and act. Here is how the apostle Paul says it to Timothy his protégé.

Train yourself to be godly. 1 Timothy 4:7

Training makes a difference, but what should men be trained to do? Well, the answer is simple. We need to be trained to hear and act.

Foundational Activity

Listen to how Jesus says it.
"Therefore everyone who hears these words of mine and puts them into practice is like a wise man who built his house on the rock. The rain came down, the streams rose, and the winds blew and beat against that house; yet it did not fall, because it had its foundation on the rock. But everyone who hears these words of mine and does not put them into practice is like a foolish man who built his house on sand. The rain came down, the streams rose, and the winds blew and beat against that house, and it fell with a great crash." When Jesus had finished saying these things, the crowds were amazed at his teaching, because he taught as one who had authority, and not as their teachers of the law. Matthew 7:24–28

I have taught these words for years, and there is so much wisdom in what Jesus says in these few verses. You have two types of men (foolish and wise) building what appear to be two similar houses (their visible lives) but in two different locations (upon sand and upon rock). Sand and rock signify two ways in which men build their lives. The man who builds on sand *hears* and *does not take action.* The man who builds on the rock *hears* and *takes the needed action.*

And then drama rolls in–a storm–as happens in life. This storm exposes how each man built his house–or better, what the visible parts have been built upon (sand or rock). From the way Jesus tells this short story it's clear the storm is imminent from the start; the men are likely aware that their houses will be tested. And the storm (the trials of life) does indeed expose the integrity of the houses (lives) that the two men have built for themselves. While the exterior of these "houses" may look the same on the outside, the men have approached the construction in very different ways. The storm exposes how they *heard* and how they *acted.* Each man's integrity is based on how he integrates *hearing* and *action.* Of these two elements, action is essential. After all, both men heard the same message but the trials exposed the quality of their response.

Jesus is closing off the greatest sermon he would ever preach, the Sermon on the Mount. This apex of the sermon is the ultimate call to action for men. It's the challenge we must be given. How and where are you building? Are you hearing and acting, or are you hearing and doing nothing? While you can try to keep up appearances before people, pretending will only work for so long; eventually there will be a storm, and the storm will test how you've prioritized your life, exposing who you really are.

The storms of life expose whether or not we have heard and acted. Each man can only pretend for so long before his integrity is exposed.

Jesus wants men everywhere to understand that acting on what we have heard Jesus say is the linchpin to a life of deep integrity, one that will stand the test of any storm. And who does not want to enjoy such a life?

There's So Much Information: How Do I Hear & Do?

Instant access to near-limitless information has improved our lives in many ways. We can communicate with almost anyone, anywhere, any time; we can send advertisements to a more relevant audience; learning is faster, and data storage is bigger. In many cases, improvements to technology and the increase in access to information are helpful–until you want to make something elegantly simple. Then a ton of information is not helpful.

For example, we now have access to excessive amounts of Christian teaching. We can stream sermons. We can be educated online. We can look up just about any theological, apologetic, or denominational issue using a search engine. But more information in this case is not always better. Information overload complicates the learning process. Sometimes men need something that is simple, repeatable, and memorable.

We need a growth plan that's uncomplicated, a language that anyone will understand. And for goodness' sake, will someone please tell us how to hear and act from God himself! I do want to hear from my pastor, educators, and online streaming media, but my far greater need is to hear and communicate with God myself.

Men need to learn how to hear directly from God, so they know how to act.

We are going to clarify in the coming chapters how to do this. We will learn how to integrate what *Jesus says* with what *Jesus wants us to do*, using five simple activities. These five will be discussed in the following chapters and developed practically so that you can use them regularly. The goal is to make them uncomplicated and understandable for men of any age. If you are a young man, you will be able to draw from these fundamentals for the rest of your life. If you are older and have experience with these fundamentals, let's consider how to practice them at increasing levels of receptivity. No matter your physical age or level of spiritual maturity, these disciplines are what men should use as fundamental activities that ignite spiritual growth.

These fundamentals inform two aspects of our lives, the *private* and the *public*. The first two activities, prayer and scripture, are often done in private. But they are not exclusively private; they can and will be done in public as well. These disciplines enable us to hear from God, so we need to make sure we have a full understanding of how to use these tools effectively. The other three are public activities: brotherhood, accountability, and ministry. They move our private activities into public view. Faithful engagement with these activities is the means by which we overcome hesitancy, fight apathy, ward off atrophy, and spiritually engage with hearing and acting as a man of God so we can listen more effectively.

Here is a general outline of the next five chapters.

Prayer

Conversations with an unseen God.

Prayer is a fundamental activity. Men must learn to build prayer routines into the daily patterns of their lives. Prayer is an unusual activity, and many men struggle to understand how to pray. Our goal is to uncomplicate the discipline of prayer and help one another develop a clear understanding within very simple steps.

Scripture

Discover the greatest book ever written, printed, and sold.

Men want the truth, and we are on a search for it daily. God's Word is the revelation of the truth, and Jesus is the physical representation of truth. But we cannot know the truth if we don't know how to spend time in the Word and with Jesus. It's not enough to inspire a man to embrace the importance of scripture, nor is it enough to challenge him to read it—we must be taught *how* to do it. This is one of the primary ways we hear from God. We will discover a simple pattern for hearing from God's Word and acting on it.

Brotherhood

We must not avoid the brotherhood we need.

Men need relationships with other men. But most men fail to develop meaningful relationships with other men, and those few relationships that do develop tend not be undergirded with a spiritual emphasis. Men prefer to go life alone for several reasons. But the biggest reason men don't establish spiritual connections with other men is that they have never experienced a healthy spiritual relationship before. Having never had one, they don't have a clear picture of what to pursue or why they should bother. Men can go their entire lives without ever experiencing the benefit.

Accountability

Christian men may have the wrong idea about accountability.

Accountability is perhaps one of the most misunderstood practices in male spiritual relationships. I believe this is because when men hear the word accountability in a religious context, they immediately assume a negative connotation. Men need a positive and proactive approach to understanding accountability before they can hope to deploy it positively and effectively.

Ministry

Getting off the bench and into the game.

All Christian men who are accelerating their spiritual growth are involved in some form of ministry, usually something of their own invention. Nothing fires men up more than making the shift from being mentored to mentoring others. Such men are finding unique ways to use their gifts, passions, and talents for the kingdom's benefit. This can feel like a very complicated endeavor, but I hope to make it simple and understandable.

Mastering these fundamentals and practicing them, not just pondering them, will help you steadily grow and mature in your spiritual life. Remember: abiding in Christ is not a passive activity. We have to engage, and the way we do this is through self-imposed disciplines. These five disciplines have the potential to accelerate spiritual growth, but more than that, they are tools for building a vibrant relationship with the God of the universe.

If you really want to dig into this content, then read the next five chapters along with the **Called To Act: 35-Day Challenge**. This challenge incorporates the teaching of each of these chapters with small daily activities that you can do *on your own* or with *a group of men*. Each challenge can be done in 5 minutes or less each day, and each has its own webpage complete with an audio file and a comment wall where you can respond to the activities, leaving comments and questions for the group. If you want to join the challenge, go to this page of my website:

www.beresolute.org/called-to-act

If you're ready, let's go on a journey of growth together.

8

Prayer

We talked about some of our experiences, focusing, hanging together down the stretch, important games. It's not necessarily who has the most talent but what team sticks together and executes their fundamentals the best.

TONY DUNGY

There are fundamentals of every concept under the sun: fundamentals of football, fundamentals of home construction, fundamentals of business leadership, and fundamentals of being a man of God.

Prayer is the most fundamental activity a man needs to build into the daily pattern of his life. Of the five fundamentals in this book, this one is non-negotiable–it needs to be done daily. As a man of God you simply cannot get by without prayer.

The Pew Research Center reports that about 55% of Americans pray every day.[1] I appreciate Pew Research for the great work that they have done

1 Michael Lipka. "5 Facts About Prayer." *Pew Research Center,* May 4, 2016. Retrieved from www.pewresearch.org/fact-tank/2016/05/04/5-facts-about-prayer/. Accessed Jan. 28, 2020.

over the years, but this sounds very high to me. The men I talk to daily admit they go seasons without praying: days, weeks, or even months. And honestly, I think confessing this to one another as men is needed and good, because we have to get to the bottom of the issue together.

So, why don't men pray?

Remember: there is a ton of information out there on prayer. You can find a sermon series online covering just about every facet of prayer. There are many perspectives out there on this one activity, and a quick search reveals a broad sample:

- *The Reason Why We Pray*
- *The Reason Why We Don't Pray*
- *The Relationship that Results from Prayer*
- *The Prayers of Jesus*
- *The Prayers of People in the Bible*
- *Prayer as Worship*
- *Effectual Prayer*
- *Doubting Prayer*
- *Intercessory Prayer*

I'm sure some of this information is helpful. Perhaps right now you might even feel inspired to search out one of these sermons and take a listen. But information about prayer does not by itself lead to transformation. As readily accessible as this information is, it has not shifted the trend of our prayer habits. Otherwise we would see a lot more people praying. So we have to ask the question again:

Why are men not praying?

If it's not about the amount of information we have, maybe it's a motivational issue. There are a variety of motivational obstacles for men. It could be that we have a superficial belief about prayer. Or maybe it's that our human ingenuity still outweighs our need for spiritual reliance. Perhaps we have low spiritual self-discipline or low self-discipline altogether. Maybe it is that we are discouraged, defeated, and disconnected from God. I definitely believe these can be contributing factors.

But what's the answer? Do men just need more motivation?

Actually, for a small percentage of men, more motivation might work. Some of us are motivated by understanding the particular obstacles in our way and simply need to be challenged. Some men actually change when someone gets in their face, like a boot camp drill sergeant. But this too has been tried. And if it worked, more men would be praying.

The Issue and the Answer

Instead, I think the problem is relatively simple. Perhaps too simple, leading us to pass over the best answer. I think the issue is that we've made prayer too complicated.

Prayer is very simple when you think about it. It's having a conversation with God. And I think too often the excessive information on prayer available to us prevents us from teaching the basics of prayer. Notice even the first followers had this same question of Jesus.

> *One day Jesus was praying in a certain place. When he finished, one of his disciples said to him, "Lord, teach us to pray, just as John taught his disciples."* Luke 11:1

These men were hungry to learn. They caught Jesus praying, liked what they saw, and they asked him to teach them. Jesus responded by praying one of the most familiar prayers in the world—the Lord's Prayer. And if you come from a liturgical tradition you know this prayer well. Although Jesus was willing to provide an outline for prayer, I don't think he intended this prayer to be the only prayer we should use. In fact, this whole chapter of Luke is filled with basic teaching about prayer, and Jesus made it all very simple. The men wanted an uncomplicated understanding, so he gave them one, saying, "You can talk to God at any time about anything." That's it. Luke 11 offers more detail, but here is a snippet.

> *"So I say to you: Ask and it will be given to you; seek and you will find; knock and the door will be opened to you. For everyone who asks receives; the one who seeks finds; and to the one who knocks, the door*

will be opened. "Which of you fathers, if your son asks for a fish, will give him a snake instead? Or if he asks for an egg, will give him a scorpion? If you then, though you are evil, know how to give good gifts to your children, how much more will your Father in heaven give the Holy Spirit to those who ask him!" Luke 11:9–13

I love that Jesus does this. He doesn't break the Lord's Prayer down into its distinct parts and then exegete them (while many do just this). He doesn't yell at his disciples in an effort to motivate them (while others do just this). He doesn't shame them for asking a very honest and good question (and I hope no one does this!). All he does is give the simplest answer possible, telling his disciples to make time and talk to God.

And that's what we are going to learn to do. We are going to uncomplicate the fundamental discipline of prayer while addressing two core issues that all men encounter when engaging in this activity: first, how to make the time; and second, what to talk about when we pray.

Preliminary Matters

Ten minutes spent in the presence of Christ every day, aye, two minutes, will make the whole day different.

HENRY DRUMMOND

So we are going to uncomplicate prayer. We are going to find a simple approach that will untangle the core issues we face. Our first underlying problem is that we don't make the time.

I think men want to enjoy a more fulfilling prayer life. I know I do, and I am sure I am not alone. But the first important step is not only expressing our intent to change, it's adding prayer to our schedule. Being inspired to pray more and the expression of intent to pray are not the same as actually praying. Action is what is necessary to move from intent to implementation. It is wonderful to feel inspired to pray, but we can't just sit around waiting for inspiration to move us to action, because it won't.

The construction of a vibrant prayer life requires us to build it into our daily schedule.

Prayer must be built habitually into the daily pattern of our life.

The primary problem with any discipline and fundamental activity are all the other pressing issues that keep us from praying and developing a pattern of prayer. On a daily basis, we face demands that compete for our time. Because of this, men endure long periods devoid of prayer, trusting only in human effort rather than trusting in God through prayer. Maybe we do this because these other pressing events actually made it into our schedule. But whatever the excuse, long droughts without prayer can leave men feeling physically exhausted and spiritually depleted. Since so many other things compete with spiritual fundamentals, we have to make time.

Men endure long periods devoid of prayer, trusting only in human effort rather than trusting in God through prayer.

To make time we need to *set a time* and *location.* This is quite simple, but I think we men need to be told to do this. I think we appreciate being presented with each step. Not because we are slow or stupid, but because making a plan is the actual first step to change. Motivation is not a step. Inspiration is not a step. Conviction is not a step. Determining a time is. And while we may think this is trivial, it's the most important thing we'll do when engaging in any fundamental activity. We must find some way to build the practice of prayer into the fabric of our daily life. Consider this: if you want to get in better physical shape, you have to *set a location* (perhaps a good jogging route or a nearby gym) and *set a time* that fits within your other responsibilities (this might include scheduling time with a trainer).

As a gym-goer myself, I can assure you that I do not get there naturally or accidentally. If I waited for it to just happen, I'd exercise infrequently at best. But that approach would never succeed in having a real impact on my health, or at least not a positive impact. Only by deliberately including the gym in my schedule and then going can my desire to improve my physical health actually change my behavior and outcomes.

Motivation is not a step. Inspiration is not a step. Conviction is not a step. Determining a time and location is a step—as long as you act!

And so the first step to all fundamental change is setting both a *time* and *location.* It is good to be informed about how to pray and to be motivated to grow closer to God, but the reality is that busyness and distractions will win out. Waiting for a time when everything feels right—not too tired, not too distracted, and armed with something we're itching to pray about—simply isn't a recipe for a vibrant prayer life. We might talk to God from time to time in passing, but not enough to really get to know him. Perhaps it doesn't feel spiritually inspiring to write prayer time into our calendars, but the truth is that this sort of practical planning is what we need to change our life for the better.

So how do we go about scheduling prayer?

From much personal trial and error, as well as my experience in guiding other men along in this task, here is what I recommend:

Set a Time

First, set a time.

I would start with a 5 to 10-minute duration that you repeat at the same time each day. While you may think that's very small, remember that we are trying to develop an ongoing pattern. I think too many men bite off more than they chew on duration, and then punt on the repetition when they cannot make the duration work. Just start with something small and build an effective pattern.

If you want to know what Jesus did, his repeated pattern was to pray early in the morning.

> *Very early in the morning, while it was still dark, Jesus got up, left the house and went off to a solitary place, where he prayed. Simon and his companions went to look for him, and when they found him, they exclaimed: "Everyone is looking for you!"* Mark 1:35–37

This was common for Jesus throughout his ministry. He was busy too, just like you, and maybe even busier–he was after all more popular than us. There were demands on his schedule. People always wanted more from him. But he scheduled a time, and his was early before dawn. Now his duration might have been longer than what you feel you can handle, but don't worry about that right now. You too will have times that you get lost in prayer and have an extended time with God. Take advantage of these moments when they happen, but otherwise stay focused on a pattern you can maintain.

For all practical purposes, here is what you should do. Put a recurring 5 to 10-minute appointment on your online calendar and have it repeat daily and indefinitely. Turn the alert on as well. If you don't have one, then set a daily alarm on your device. I prefer the calendar appointment because I have to look at my calendar every day. When I miss a scheduled time with God, I am going to have to stare at it, shamefully nonetheless, the rest of the day. Sometimes a little guilt can be good motivation.

I would recommend setting a time early in the morning, like Jesus did, but if this absolutely does not work for you, then set it at the time that is right for you.

Set a Location

So now that you have *set a time*, you should *set a location.*

> *Very early in the morning, while it was still dark, Jesus got up, left the house and went off to a solitary place, where he prayed. Simon and his companions went to look for him, and when they found him, they exclaimed: "Everyone is looking for you!"* Mark 1:35–37

His prayer time was early; his location was private. He left the company of other people to be in the company of God.

Keep this practical: pick a familiar and quiet location, either in your home or a convenient spot elsewhere, where you will not be interrupted. And then, daily, when prompted by your calendar, go there.

Men underestimate the focus it takes to pray. There are so many distractions, including people, devices, media, and the like. Some of these things are otherwise indispensable, but they cannot follow us into certain activities. For example, when I go to church, sit at the dinner table, or enter a meeting I turn off my phone. Why? So I can focus the way I need to during that time. Trying to practice the activity of prayer with people, devices, and media coming at us deters us from having a meaningful engagement with the experience.

You need a location and place that is all your own, where you and God can interact without interruption. (Don't worry about whether other people or responsibilities are requesting your attention. Spoiler alert: they can wait.) The environment of your location is also important, but this part is subjective. Pick a place that works best for you. This could be a quiet office, an outdoor trail, a back porch of your house, or even a quiet car ride on the way to work each day. But it needs to meet your needs and be a silent place with few distractions so that you can talk with God without constant interruption.

The P.A.C.T. Method

True prayer is measured by weight, not by length. A single groan before God may have more fullness of prayer in it than a fine oration of great length.

CHARLES SPURGEON

The second core issue we face is knowing what to talk about when we pray. In other words, what do we actually do when we get to this scheduled time?

There are a whole lot of questions that come up at this moment that many men are embarrassed to ask. And for good reason. Prayer can be complicated. We are told to talk to someone we have not seen, someone who is not visibly standing in front of us. It feels a lot like talking to ourselves. And indeed you may end up asking yourself lots of great questions.

- *What should I say?*
- *What should I not say?*
- *Can I be mad when I talk, or do I have to wait until I've got my emotions under control?*
- *Which person do I pray to: God the Father, Jesus, or the Holy Spirit?*
- *Does God not want to hear me talk about certain topics?*
- *Is there a certain way to start and finish?*
- *What if I forget to say something?*
- *What should my physical posture be?*
- *Do I have to close my eyes, or can I pray with my eyes open?*
- *I have seen other people pray who seem to have a lot to say. What if I cannot come up with anything?*

I have asked all of these myself, yet most of the time we are afraid to ask for fear of looking incompetent or feeling stupid. But they are valid questions. I tell men to begin with this four-part acronym—P.A.C.T.

Pray Out Loud

> *Going a little farther, he fell with his face to the ground and prayed, "My Father, if it is possible, may this cup be taken from me. Yet not as I will, but as you will."* Matthew 26:39

I think Jesus had a dual motive whenever he prayed. While he was indeed concerned with connecting with the Father, he also meant to teach his followers by letting them watch his example. I think most people miss this detail, but notice what happens above (and in many other places in the Gospels). Matthew, the author, describes Jesus praying in the garden. Yes, Matthew offers us the visual details: Jesus has fallen with his face in the dirt. But notice the other sensory detail—Matthew records what Jesus was praying. Which means Matthew could *hear* Jesus praying. Why? Because Jesus *prayed out loud.*

This is the first principle: *pray out loud.*

I think many men fail at their scheduled time of prayer because they pray exclusively in their heads or hearts. If Jesus had done this, no one would have been able to write down anything he prayed. Thankfully, Jesus was willing to model his prayer life for his disciples—and for us. His actions demonstrated what prayer *looks* and *sounds* like. He did it not to put on a show; he knew that an abstract activity such as prayer is best understood by listening to others, and therefore he allowed his men to listen in and learn.

In my life, I have found when I pray out loud, I am much more focused. I have to form sentences, ideas, and complete thoughts, and I stay with prayer longer. If you don't want to pray out loud, prayer journaling is very effective, too, because it requires you to express yourself coherently in the same way. But even if you choose to write out your prayers in a prayer journal, speaking out loud in a time of prayer is super-helpful. It does take some time to get used to, and I admit I have been awkwardly interrupted a few times by my wife and kids, but I am sure they are better for catching me as I was talking with God.

When men pray out loud, they are much more focused, and are required to form complete thoughts.

Notice the relationship that Moses had with God:

The Lord would speak to Moses face to face, as one speaks to a friend.
Exodus 33:11

I love this short explanatory sentence in the Old Testament book of Exodus. It captures what I think God wants to have with every man: a real conversational relationship. So start talking out loud to God. If your prayer location discourages that practice, find a better spot.

Ask God

> *"Therefore I tell you, whatever you ask for in prayer, believe that you have received it, and it will be yours."* Mark 11:24

> *"And whatever you ask in prayer, you will receive, if you have faith."* Matthew 21:22

> *"If you abide in me, and my words abide in you, ask whatever you wish, and it will be done for you."* John 15:7

> *"Whatever you ask in my name, this I will do, that the Father may be glorified in the Son."* John 14:3

> *"Ask, and it will be given to you; seek, and you will find; knock, and it will be opened to you."* Matthew 7:7

Jesus had a lot to say about making requests in prayer. Make sure you read all of his teachings above. They seem almost preposterous when grouped together like this. It's as if Jesus is daring us to ask and see the benefit.

In our prayer time we should feel free to ask, to be honest with God about what we desire to know and receive. Spend less time worrying about what you are asking, and more time just asking. I often catch myself throughout the day thinking about things I should pray about rather than actually taking the time to pray about them–and then I forget to do it later.

Spend less time worrying about what to ask God, and just ask. Jesus dares men to ask.

I would suggest starting with only one thing to ask God and then invest multiple days on this one thing. You might even keep a list in a journal of what you are asking for and why, or you might share the list with someone you trust. As you pray, *watch*: over time he will answer these prayers in a lot of unique and interesting ways.

If you have a hard time coming up with items to pray about, consider one item in one of the 5-F categories: *faith*, *family*, *finance*, *fitness*, and *friendships*. Don't do one in all five; this would quickly become overwhelming. As you begin to pray just stick with one. This is a great place to start as you try to identify the heaviest concerns in your life.

Confess to God

> *Therefore confess your sins to each other and pray for each other so that you may be healed. The prayer of a righteous person is powerful and effective.* James 5:16

Confession is not a word we use much, but its meaning is relatively simple. Its literal meaning in the context of prayer is *"agreeing with God."* So, when we confess during a prayer time, we are *agreeing with God* about what he already knows. This is a place in prayer where our honesty, openness, and transparency come into play.

The most honest, open, and transparent relationship we will ever have is the one we have with God. He is a father who knows everything, and because he does, there is no need to hide from him. We need to talk with him about the things he already knows that often he just wants us to honestly acknowledge.

We keep coming back to this situation, but in Genesis 3, God was looking for man to be honest, open, and transparent with him about his sin. During the dialogue (again, notice it is *out loud*) God questions man, and man responds:

> *Then the man and his wife heard the sound of the Lord God as he was walking in the garden in the cool of the day, and they hid from the Lord God among the trees of the garden. But the Lord God called to the man, "Where are you?"*
> *He answered, "I heard you in the garden, and I was afraid because I was naked; so I hid."*

> *And he said, "Who told you that you were naked? Have you eaten from the tree that I commanded you not to eat from?"*
> *The man said, "The woman you put here with me—she gave me some fruit from the tree, and I ate it."* Genesis 3:8–12

I think it's laughable that man responds this way. He blames woman–a backhanded way of blaming God–rather than confessing his failure. Yet God had given him opportunity to be honest, open, and transparent and to confess what he did. God was daring him to *go there*, but instead Adam hid.

There is really no need to hide from God. He knows everything, anyway. And the best conversations I've had with God are moments of confession. They are full of emotion, and they are the moments when I feel free in my relationship with God. The most daring prayers by a man are these moments he comes clean in confession to God. Take this one by David after his adulterous affair with Bathsheba.

> *When I kept silent, my bones wasted away through my groaning all day long. For day and night your hand was heavy on me; my strength was sapped as in the heat of summer. Then I acknowledged my sin to you and did not cover up my iniquity. I said, "I will confess my transgressions to the Lord." And you forgave the guilt of my sin.*
> Psalm 32:3-5

Each time I read these words, I am reminded of two things. First, that David said these words *out loud* and turned them into a *public song*. Second, that every honest, open, and transparent man who readily makes confession has an intimate trust relationship with God and others.

The most daring prayers by a man are the moments he comes clean in confession to God.

If you are looking for something to confess and are unsure of what to share with God, again consider one, not all, of those 5-F categories:

faith, *family*, *finance*, *fitness*, and *friendships*. Just do this: reflect on the last 24 hours and search for a moment in which you might have caused harm to someone or something in one of these categories. Then be specific with God about what you did, what you should have done, and what you would like to do better in the future. I have found by addressing specific mistakes, and not general sinfulness, that I have lots to talk with God about. Let's be honest, we all frequently fumble in some areas. Besides, God already knows the mistakes we've made; confession just heightens our awareness of how we need to realign ourselves with God.

Thank God

> *Devote yourselves to prayer, being watchful and thankful.*
> Colossians 4:2

We need to tell God, *"Thank You."*

I will frequently devote entire prayers to thanking God. I need to make this deliberate choice because I often get lost in myself during prayer time, only asking God for what I want and need. But God deserves *thanks* and praise for what he has done. God loves our praise, and while he does not need it, this does not mean we should not do it.

In the Bible there is a story that directly addresses this issue. Here is how it reads.

> *Now on his way to Jerusalem, Jesus traveled along the border between Samaria and Galilee. As he was going into a village, ten men who had leprosy met him. They stood at a distance and called out in a loud voice, "Jesus, Master, have pity on us!"*
> *When he saw them, he said, "Go, show yourselves to the priests." And as they went, they were cleansed.*
> *One of them, when he saw he was healed, came back, praising God in a loud voice. He threw himself at Jesus' feet and thanked him—and he was a Samaritan.*
> *Jesus asked, "Were not all ten cleansed? Where are the other nine? Has no one returned to give praise to God except this foreigner?" Then he said to him, "Rise and go; your faith has made you well."*

Luke 17:11–19

This is a near perfect example of thankfulness. God is frequently and incessantly generous to man, yet few (in this case only a small percentage) take time to give him thanks. And while Jesus in this situation is not sustained by our thankfulness, he wants us to do it primarily for our benefit.

Part of praying is thanking God so that our mind is reminded, our heart is submissive, and our soul finds sustenance in God. It's the part of the conversation where we get to celebrate with God not because he needs it, but because we do. It keeps us in faithful submission to God.

Men need to thank God, not because he need its, but we need to be reminded and give recognition of his work in our daily life.

Again, if you struggle with content, reach for those 5-F categories—*faith*, *family*, *finance*, *fitness*, and *friendships*. Find one thing in your life to really focus on and then thank God for it.

Now Put It All Together

Each of the four parts we've laid out help to balance our time in conversation with God. It will take time to work this out, but each of these parts should help you to build a vibrant and balanced prayer time. If you don't include all four elements every time you pray, that's okay; sometimes all you will do is *ask* or *confess* or express *thanks*, but each should find its way into your regular prayer life. Use the P.A.C.T. acronym to help you format the time, but more than anything, simply remember to talk out loud with God. There is no activity more vital in a man's life than the time he invests with God in prayer. These will be private and powerful moments.

As you stick with it, you will come to realize that your prayer conversation is continuing throughout the day. It will evolve in your heart, shape your thinking, inform your action, and awaken you to the things of

God. As you become settled in the daily rhythm, you will discover more of your day taking on a *prayerful attitude*, rather than merely utilizing a prayer method. This captures what I think Paul meant to convey here:

> *Rejoice always, pray continually, give thanks in all circumstances; for this is God's will for you in Christ Jesus.* 1 Thessalonians 5:16–18

Through faithful discipline, you will discover this kind of continuity in prayer, but you can get started with the simple habits suggested, and then scale up as you go. You will get there; just give it time to become habitual. And always remember: prayer is only a means to an end, the end being a vibrant relationship with Christ.

> Prayer makes a godly man, and puts within him the mind of Christ, the mind of humility, of self-surrender, of service, of pity, and of prayer. If we really pray, we will become more like God, or else we will quit praying.
>
> **E.M. BOUNDS**

Reflection & Discussion Questions

1. How frequently do you pray?
2. What obstacles prevent you from investing time in prayer?
3. What do you say in a typical prayer?
4. How do you think your life would be different with consistent prayer?

Call to Action

The following steps are your call to action in the area of prayer. Take a few minutes to determine your time and location, and then practice the discipline of prayer on your own or with another man.

1 | Preliminary Matters:

- **Set a Time:** *Start with 5-10 minutes and set a recurring calendar appointment. What's your time?*
- **Set a Location:** *Find somewhere you can go that is quiet and alone. What's your best location?*

2 | The P.A.C.T. Method:

- **Pray Out Loud:** *Literally talk out loud, not in your head.*
- **Ask:** *Make a list of 1–3 things to ask God. What's on your list?*
- **Confess:** *Agree with God and be honest, open, and transparent with him. What do you need to confess?*
- **Thank:** *Make a list of 3–5 things to thank God for in your life. What's on your list?*
- *Leverage the 5-F categories as needed: faith, family, finance, fitness, and friendships.*

Remember: if you are looking for help in stepping through this daily, join the **35-Day Challenge** online at **www.beresolute.org/called-to-act**.

9

Scripture

It ain't those parts of the Bible that I can't understand that bother me, it is the parts that I do understand.

MARK TWAIN

We are always on the lookout for a memorable, life-changing experience. Men will stand in line to catch a blockbuster movie, hear a great musician, watch a great play, experience an exciting new ride, or attend a marquee sporting event. In addition, we will pay the parking fees and buy some of the seriously overpriced concessions at the event. It's all part of the experience.

But men have a hard time reading the Bible. We do try. Some will try many times. But we are often overwhelmed when we try. We might buy a Bible, or two, or three–and they will sit on the shelf. According to the American Bible Society almost nine out of ten households own a Bible, and the average household has three, but only 37 percent of people read it once a week or more. Research from the Barna Group reports that people don't read the Bible for several reasons, but top two on the list are because they don't have enough time or struggle to relate to the language.

Yet this dust-collecting book contains the greatest stories ever told. The Bible is filled with love, war, birth, and death. It reveals to us an ancient culture, one rich with poetry, history, philosophy, and science. The Bible combines mystery, romance, suspense, thriller, action, and adventure–and it even has a book with a strong parental advisory because of its explicit sexual content.

The Bible has things to say about money. It has things to say about some of the hottest controversies of our time. Politics, government, and the church: the Bible dives into conversation topics you avoid at your Thanksgiving table. It is full of hundreds of prophecies that came true. It is full of scientific ideas that very smart people are still discovering. It describes many archeological artifacts that we are still trying to find, and plenty that we already have. In 1455 it became the first book ever printed on the printing press, and today it continues to be the best-selling and most distributed book of all time, with an estimated 5 billion copies sold. New copies are being produced at a volume of about 100 million each year. To put those numbers in perspective, the #2 bestselling book all time is *A Tale of Two Cities* by Charles Dickens with 200 million total copies sold and distributed.

Clearly this book is worth reading for its cultural value alone. And of course it is far more valuable than that. We all understand the importance of the Bible, and we all want to be able to read and understand the scriptures. But what I have come to learn is that the Bible seems overly complicated for us men. And when something gets complicated for a man, he punts on engagement. But we cannot afford to respond this way because reading the Bible is how we hear from God and learn to act like men.

When it comes to the Bible, many of us are afraid to admit we don't know what to do. The first step stumps us, and we stall out. We're like the man lost for direction and unsure where to go; yet we won't stop and ask for directions. And the reasons why we don't: self-sufficiency and shame. Men are overly self-sufficient, believing they can try to just figure it out on their own; in some cases, men are too ashamed to admit they need guidance and therefore never ask for help. So this chapter is devoted to that one activity that we won't seek guidance for. Let's unpack the answer to our unspoken question: *How do I read scripture?*

What's Complicated About Scripture?

Well just about everything is. Most men are unwilling to admit this because they don't want to appear ignorant or be offensive, but everything about scripture is complicated. Here are the top questions that men of almost any physical or spiritual age have asked me when they pick up the Bible.

Which Version Do I Choose?

Over my lifetime, I have led hundreds of men to Christ. And one of the first things I used to do when we had bookstores (remember those?) was to walk a guy over to the religion section and help him pick out his first Bible. This is a tricky process. You can't just grab a copy and move on because, depending on the store, there may be hundreds of choices. It's overwhelming. Hundreds of versions of one book. Who knew, right?

You'll find study Bibles, archaeological Bibles, devotional Bibles, men's Bibles, patriotic Bibles, teen Bibles, and even the "word on the street" urban Bibles. Then you realize that these represent many different translations of scripture, often denoted by their abbreviations: New International Version (NIV); English Standard Version (ESV); New Living Translation (NLT), and so on. And there are more than a hundred of these.

So what's up with this? Here is the skinny.

Scripture was originally written in two different languages. The first part of the Bible was written in the Hebrew language, and the Greek language was used in the second part of the Bible. Groups of language scholars have formed teams and translated the Bible from its original two languages into other languages (like English) to give the Bible a more modern understanding. Of course, this has been done many times, mainly for three recurring reasons.

- *Language is always evolving.*
- *Discoveries are always being made.*
- *Different scholars have different approaches to translation.*

For example, "selfie" was not a word at one point in history, but then some teenagers took a picture of themselves and, presto, we have a new word. Or, we discover something like the Dead Sea Scrolls we now have additional evidence that leads to more precise translations. But I want to focus in particular on the last reason above because it is very important.

When translating, each team of scholars that is working together has to make a choice on how they are going to translate scripture. We can reduce their options to these three approaches:

- *Word for Word (usually translated one word at a time)*
- *Thought for Thought (usually translated one phrase or thought at a time)*
- *Paraphrase (usually translated a paragraph at a time)*

There are more technical words that scholars use for these concepts, but this a fair analysis. With this in mind, you can now categorize all those abbreviations into these three categories.

The Word-for-Word translations like the ESV (English Standard Version), KJV (King James Version), and RSV (Revised Standard Version) all follow this literal-minded format. Translation teams are attempting to rely as heavily as possible on the original text, leaving the work of interpretation to the reader. Some people like this approach because they would rather study for themselves and dig out the original feel and meaning. The drawback is that it can feel awkward to read at times. Ideally, to benefit from these translations you should be skilled at interpretation or finding historical answers.

The Thought-for-Thought translations like the NIV (New International Version), NLT (New Living Translation), and the GNT (Good News Translation) all follow a more reader-friendly format. Translation teams are attempting to follow a format that conveys meaning for today that has high readability. This means you'll have to trust the translation team a little more because they are going to do some of the interpretation for you. But you shouldn't need to struggle as much to understand what you're reading.

The Paraphrase translations are few. They are just that: a simple paraphrase. The most popular of these is *The Message,* which was written not by a team but a single author, Eugene Peterson. It's poetic writing, and he takes a lot of liberty in his rendition. Given the subjective interpretation involved on the part of the author, I would not recommend using a paraphrase version for personal study. It's also worth noting that paraphrase translations are less popular overall, so you may feel out of place using one of these Bibles in a group setting.

Where Do I Start Reading?

This is another fair and honest question. Typically, we start at the beginning of a book when we read. But the Bible is no ordinary book. It has a lot of different types of literature within it. It has romance (Song of Solomon), history (Genesis), religious law (Leviticus), conquest (Joshua), drama (Job), prophecy (Isaiah), wisdom (Proverbs), songs (Psalms), letters (Romans), apocalypse (Revelation), and books containing Jesus's life and ministry (the "gospels:" Matthew, Mark, Luke, and John). Given this variety of material, we do *not* have to start right at the beginning. We can think of the Bible more like a library. Go ahead and start anywhere, selecting a book that has a type of literature that you find compelling.

One great place to start is with one of the four Gospels. Gospel is an Old English word meaning *"good news."* The four books of good news are Matthew, Mark, Luke, and John; these describe the life and ministry of Jesus Christ. Each of these books was written by a different author at a different time, which helps you see Jesus's life and ministry from different perspectives.

After reading one or all of the four Gospels, then I would say any and everything in the Bible is fair game. The key is simply to start reading and *keep* reading.

What's with the Structure?

This is another great question I get, so here is a simple answer.

Think of it as a big book of history with a library of books within it. It had 40 different authors and was written over a period of about 2,000 years. The Bible has two major sections, the Old and New Testament. Don't get hung up on the word Testament; it just means, "A covenant made between God and man." Maybe think of it as Part One and Part Two. Now, when you hear the word "old," some people assume this means "no longer valid," which would be an incorrect assessment of the Old Testament. The Bible is one whole story, and the themes driving all the way through it are still valid today.

The Old Testament is the original Hebrew Bible. The addition of the New Testament came after Jesus lived, died, and rose again. This completed the story about the Messiah, who was prophesied about in the Old Testament. Thanks to those prophecies, the entire Bible tells one story of God's love and redemption of man through his Son, Jesus Christ. The life of Jesus is the primary metanarrative that ties all of scripture together. Every story, every moment, and every tension culminate in the life, death, and resurrection of Jesus Christ.

For sake of awareness, here is how the 66 books of the Bible may be categorized.

The Old Testament: (39 Books)

- *Law:* Genesis, Exodus, Leviticus, Numbers, Deuteronomy
- *History:* Joshua, Judges, Ruth, 1-2 Samuel, 1-2 Kings, 1-2 Chronicles, Ezra, Nehemiah, Esther
- *Poetry/Wisdom:* Job, Psalms, Proverbs, Ecclesiastes, The Song of Solomon
- *Prophets:* Isaiah, Jeremiah, Lamentations, Ezekiel, Daniel, Hosea, Joel, Amos, Obadiah, Jonah, Micah, Nahum, Habakkuk, Zephaniah, Haggai, Zechariah, Malachi

The New Testament: (27 Books)

- *Gospels:* Matthew, Mark, Luke, John
- *History:* Acts
- *Letters:* Romans, 1-2 Corinthians, Galatians, Ephesians, Philippians, Colossians, 1-2 Thessalonians, 1-2 Timothy, Titus, Philemon, Hebrews, James, 1-2 Peter, 1-3 John, Jude
- *Prophetic:* Revelation

This structure gives you a bit of map for finding books to read and even learning how to read them.

Why Are the Language, Customs, and Names So Complicated to Understand?

Yep, this part of reading scripture is complicated. Lest we forget, this is an ancient Near Eastern historical document. Remember that the authors of the individual books above wrote to distinctive groups of people in distinctive places in a time long past. These authors were writing to people in their own time and could presume their readers would know specific cultural details. Since we don't live in that time and don't necessarily know those details, interpretation is a bigger challenge for us. And this is largely what makes reading scripture complicated.

Our inability to share in the original readership's assumed understanding of cultural application is the core issue we must resolve in order to effectively read scripture. We certainly have the tools we need to surmount this obstacle, but most men today struggle to read with that level of focus. When (or if) a man does read, most of what he reads has been written with his cultural context in mind. It is usually delivered in a way that is convenient for him to access, which makes for an easy and fast transition into application. This is ideal for how we are wired. We like easy, not because we are slow or stupid, but because we like moving into action. From the moment we are called to act, we are ready to go. We prefer to skip all the preliminary stuff, like reading the directions, and want to jump right into assembling the swing set, the toilet, or the IKEA bookshelf. I feel the same impulses. But reading scripture requires a little more work than reading a sports article or popular magazine. And because it does, men punt on it.

But I want to uncomplicate this for you in such a way that will keep you coming back for more every day. We need to turn the Bible from the best selling, most distributed, and *least* read book into the best selling, most distributed, and *most* read book by men. Why? Because to be men who are called to act, we have to hear. And the person we need to hear from is God.

The P.A.S.S. Method

I am profitably engaged in reading the Bible. Take all of this Book that you can by reason and the balance by faith, and you will live and die a better man. It is the best Book which God has given to man.

ABRAHAM LINCOLN

I want to show you how to draw something meaningful from scripture every time you read, and despite the few obstacles, I believe you can do this. In the last chapter on developing a discipline of prayer, you learned that the first thing you need to do is determine a time and location. To fully benefit from reading scripture, you're going to need to do the same thing: you've got to carve out a daily slot in your calendar, and you need to select an environment suitable for focused reading. If your goal is to read the Bible regularly, clearing time and space is only half the battle, you won't be able to stay motivated if you can't understand what you read. But once you learn how to discern God's voice within these ancient words, you'll keep coming back for more.

I want to share with you the P.A.S.S. method of study. This method is outlined in the next four steps, and I know that if you follow each of them, then you will discover some amazing benefits while listening to God in the scripture.

Pray Prior to Reading

In the beginning was the Word, and the Word was with God, and the Word was God. He was with God in the beginning....
The Word became flesh and made his dwelling among us. We have seen his glory, the glory of the one and only Son, who came from the Father, full of grace and truth. John 1:1–2, 14

There is one major characteristic that differentiates scripture from every other book. This factor alone is the most important reason to read scripture daily. As John testifies above, this is a living document. The very words of God became a living being in Jesus Christ. The fancy word for this is *"incarnate,"* which means *"with flesh."* (Just think chili con carne: chili with meat.) Jesus was with God and came from heaven to be God's Word made human. The visual here is both strange and powerful, and it conveys that God's Word (Jesus) is the ever-living, ever-present self-disclosure of God.

This is what makes scripture unique. It is revelation by God and about God so that we can know God. Scripture supernaturally reveals truth and power to those who read it. The Bible is not static writing like all other books. When we read this book, we're reading something that is a revelation from the mouth of a timeless God. No other book claims such a thing. Not one.

After Jesus arrives on the scene and begins his ministry, he testifies to everything written and talked about in the Old Testament. He supports its teachings, gives evidence of his authority, and speaks on behalf of God. He himself says this:

> *"For the works that the Father has given me to finish—the very works that I am doing—testify that the Father has sent me."* John 5:36

And finally the apostle Paul states this about scripture:

> *All Scripture is God-breathed and is useful for teaching, rebuking, correcting and training in righteousness, so that the man of God may be thoroughly equipped for every good work.* 2 Timothy 3:16–17

Notice Paul calls scripture *"breathed"* by God. To use modern language, scripture is *"inspired"* by God. Yes, by God and not man. We know that scripture was written down by men, but all men, even the biblical authors, were fallible, sinful, and fallen men like you and me. However, God entrusted them to communicate and write down his Word as directed; therefore his Word is indeed inspired. Scripture is the very breath of God, and it leads men along the path of life by

- Teaching–*showing us the path;*
- Rebuking–*showing us when we are off the path;*
- Correcting–*showing us how to get back on the path; and*
- Training–*showing us how to stay on the path.*

Since this book is an incredible resource for truth and change, it's essential to approach this book with prayer and reverence. Not because we worship the Bible. There's a word for that: *bibliolatry*. No: we worship the God of the Bible whose inspired Word has power to change a man's life even today, thousands of years after it was first written.

I encourage men to always pray prior to reading scripture. Pray that God would help you hear what he wants you to hear so you can be the man he wants you to be. This is where you have the opportunity to do some spadework in the parts of your life that are hard, rocky, and thorny. The preferred outcome is multiplied produce, as Jesus stated in the Parable of the Sower, and this requires a reverent approach to scripture and an expectant heart. Trust that God wants to change your thoughts, actions, and motives through what you are about to read–and invite him to do so. This prayer is the first step to the P.A.S.S. method, and it should take place before you read a single word.

When reading scripture, men should approach it as an divinely inspired document. The Bible is a living document, it's not like other books. Read it as such–prayerfully.

Acknowledge Author Intent

Next, as you begin to read, remember that you have to read a little differently. You have to read with intent.

Most read the Bible with a narrow focus of just trying to complete the passage. After all, reading scripture can feel like work, painful work. It's hard because the original author assumed his reader would understand all of his cultural references and thus arrive promptly at the intended application.

Perhaps that was a safe assumption at one time, but this is certainly no longer the case. Compared to the earliest readers, scripture requires us to do a little more work to discover its full context; we have to tune in our attention and intention.

Let me put this simply: *the Bible was not written to you.*

Now, this is a bit of an overstatement, but I want you to remember this point because it's critical in learning to read scripture. Let me say it again with a small clarification: "The Bible was not written *to* you, but it was written *for* you."

The Bible was not written to you, but it was written for you, so acknowledge the author's intent.

So who was the Bible written to?

Well, the primary audience of each book in the Bible is the group to whom it was first written; let's call these respective groups the first audience. Each author had a particular intent for writing his book and a particular recipient (first audience) in mind for that message.

For example, when we read Matthew's Gospel, which is the first book of the New Testament, we should understand that Matthew was writing down what he witnessed, heard, and experienced as he followed the life, death, and resurrection of Jesus. I doubt he realized that 2,000 years later we would still be reading his book. Initially, he wanted the people of his day, specifically his Christian brothers of Jewish heritage, to have a record of evidence about Christ, who was both man and God; Matthew pointed to his life ministry as an act of God. This book was evidence for believers in his day and time. Is Matthew's book inspired by God? Of course, but it's written from the perspective of this man to his first audience. This means that the author's intent is critical to identify. As we read scripture, we need to take out our detective kit and search for what the author intended to say about God to that first audience.

This principle is the key to understanding what we read, and it is the key to finding a valid application. Without acknowledging the author's intent, we may wrongly interpret what we read in the text. Yet if we know the author's intent, our understanding and application will be sounder.

So we need to figure out why the author was writing and what he wanted his first readers to learn about God. Let's phrase that as a simple question:

What does this author want his people to know about God?

This one question will help you approach and engage scripture differently. It will help you to read with more intention, much like a detective searching for truth.

Stop When You're Convicted

The next step in reading scripture is to pay little mind to the amount of reading you do each time. I think that some men feel like they need to consume certain amounts of the text each time in order to feel accomplished, or to keep up with a reading schedule of some kind. Honestly, I think it's unhelpful to worry about this; remember, this is not a reading contest.

I should clarify that there is nothing wrong with trying to read through the Bible in a year–it's a worthy goal–but consuming large amounts of information does not always lead to transformation. And I believe men feel equally if not more accomplished and successful by consuming small quantities and receiving quality results from the experience. It will keep them coming back for more, and for the right reason. In the New Testament Jesus had strong things to say to the religious teachers who knew a lot about the teaching of God yet did little to implement the teachings in their own lives. So maybe it's time to worry less about the quantity of your reading and more about quality of your conviction and change.

This is what I tell men to do next: Choose a book of the Bible to read and start with a chapter. Read just one chapter a day. If needed, read it multiple times, but stop as soon as you feel personally convicted by something in the text.

Yep. Just stop.

I have found that whenever I read scripture, I experience moments of conviction. I used to skip right past them, but then one day I stopped and prayed. This moment turned into an incredible experience between God and me. What I quite naturally did was combine prayer and scripture when I was prompted by a conviction of the Holy Spirit. In this moment, I discovered something I had never been taught or encouraged to do by any mentor, teacher, pastor, or leader in my entire life. I discovered that God uses his living Word to speak directly to me, so that it produces change in my life. Throughout all the years up until then, I had skipped over these nudges because I was focused on completing my quota.

Let's take a look at what Jesus said about the work of the Holy Spirit:

> *"When [the Holy Spirit] comes, he will prove the world to be in the wrong about sin and righteousness and judgment."* John 16:8

This is precisely what happened to me. So, when I instruct men to read scripture I tell them to stop when they feel one of the three convictions:

- *A conviction about something they should* ***stop***
- *A conviction about something they should* ***start***
- *A conviction about something they should* ***continue***

I have read entire books of the Bible this way, and it is a life-changing exercise. The end goal of reading scripture should be to experience change within our hearts and to become equipped for the work to which we are called.

Let's take a second look at Paul's message to Timothy regarding the purpose of scripture:

> *So that the man of God may be thoroughly equipped for every good work.* 2 Timothy 3:17

We become changed and get equipped when we allow the Spirit to convict. It's one conviction, one day, and one scripture at a time. Ultimately, this is a conviction that God is the truth and we are not, that God's way is *the* way, and our way is not always *his* way. But each time we read scripture, we discover small convictions regarding our motives, thoughts, attitudes, and actions. Most of these convictions will by nature be reactive, meaning that we are convicted of some manner of sin in the recent past. Therefore, when we read scripture daily, we give more opportunities for God's truth to convict us, for his Spirit to work on us, and for truth to shape us. These daily convictions reveal the steps we need to take to become more proactive and more perfectly reflect God in this life.

Conviction reminds us that God's way is the way, and our way is not always his way.

Therefore, every time I read scripture I'm looking for something that convicts me. Something that God wants me to address in my life. Usually, after I have prayed and have identified the author's intent, God hits me with a conviction. He *"speaks"* directly to me. I mostly experience this as a stray thought during a momentary reflection. It's a stray thought that says something like this:

- *"I am bothered by this feeling, motivation, attitude, or action."*
- *"I need to deal with this feeling, motivation, attitude, or action."*
- *"I am not doing that godly action often enough."*

In this moment I usually stop reading immediately. While I impulsively want to get through the reading, I need to stop. Immediately. Just linger for a moment. I'll grab scratch paper, a journal, or sticky note and jot down what I'm thinking. Then I'll spend some time in prayer, pausing again to reflect on what I want to stop, start, or continue.

Share Scripture with Others

Now, when some men hear me say, *"Share scripture with others,"* they immediately get overwhelmed. Typically they think I am asking them to memorize a verse and recite it to others (and this is a great idea that's worth the investment of time) but this is not what I am talking about. What I mean by sharing scripture is finding great concepts within the scripture you are reading and then carrying them with you throughout your day. Worry less about sharing the exact words and more about sharing what you have learned from the text.

Share the truth of scripture by sharing each day something you have learned from reading God's Word.

If you want scripture to stick with you or alter how you act, then you need to start sharing what you've learned. Focus on the principles and lessons that come from those moments of conviction. Some days this might look like sharing the general principle; on other days this might mean sharing the exact words of the verse. Some guys feel relatively comfortable in their home and work environments and have no problem talking about the general principles they have read. Others will need to muster up the nerve. But it's worth making the effort. Go after it! You might bring the principle up in a meeting, share the thought with a friend, or text what you've learned to someone you care about: a friend, spouse, or child. When we know that we are going to share scripture with others, we read it differently. Today, I challenge you to look for something that captures your attention as you read; something that feels worthy of talking about that might connect you to the people you will interact with.

This is just one way we move from hearing to acting on scripture: first we *get it out*, and then *we live it out.*

It's Your Turn

So now it's your turn. Start diving in, not only into prayer but now scripture as well. This is precisely how I started writing the **Men's Daily Devotional** (www.beresolute.org/mdd). I use the same process mentioned here to find things daily in scripture worthy of sharing with other men. It might help you to read and then just watch how I do it for a while till you get in the rhythm. Men just like you read these thoughts every day. Perhaps like you, they struggle when they read scripture and just want a little help. So give it a try. Every insight I post there is a result of prayer, acknowledging the author's intent, stopping when convicted, and sharing God's message to the world.

> *So Jesus said to the Jews who had believed him, "If you abide in my word, you are truly my disciples, and you will know the truth, and the truth will set you free."* John 8:31–32

Reflection & Discussion Questions

1. Other than the Bible what book you have read during your lifetime that has had a lasting impact on your life?
2. How often do you currently read the Bible? Be honest.
3. What is the first book of the Bible you recall reading? Why did you start with that book?
4. What is challenging about reading the Bible regularly?
5. What is one thing you've discovered in your Bible reading that has left a lasting impression on your life?

Call to Action

The following steps are your call to action in the area of scripture. Take a few minutes to select a section of scripture to study in the coming days or weeks. For example, consider an easy to read New Testament book like the book of James. Select a short section (3-6 verses) from one of the chapters and then try using the P.A.S.S Method.

The P.A.S.S. Method:

- **Pray:** *prior to reading. Stop and pray.*
- **Acknowledge:** *author intent. What is the author intent in this text?*
- **Stop:** *when you feel convicted. What convicted you in this text?*
- **Share:** *what you learn. What principle can you share with others today? Write it down.*

If you want help using the P.A.S.S. method, consider following along with me on the **35-Day Challenge** that pairs with this book. I will guide you through a book of the Bible and help you study scripture over a number of days, step-by-step using the principles above. Check it out online at www.beresolute.org/called-to-act.

10

Brotherhood

Two are better than one, because they have a good return for their labor: If either of them falls down, one can help the other up. But pity anyone who falls and has no one to help them up. Ecclesiastes 4:9–10

Since men consume books at different rates of speed, I want to encourage you to keep moving forward with the previous two activities in chapters eight and nine. If you are using this book in conjunction with the **35-Day Challenge**, you should be following along daily and reading through one chapter each week. During the challenge, we devote seven days to each of these topics to help you build them into the daily pattern of your life.

If you are not doing the **35-Day Challenge**, you might just be reading through this book in a few sittings, so let me underscore that the practice and regular application of the previous two disciplines should be a part of a daily experience, not merely a reading experience. Remember, information does not always lead to transformation, but changed behavior does. You can accomplish much of we have discussed in about five minutes each day. Once you get the practice down in a daily rhythm, you will experience the greatest benefit.

Now we are going to make a subtle shift.

The previous two activities are things we usually practice on our own. Many dub them private practices. But I think a better word to characterize the nature of prayer and scripture reading is personal. We engage in these disciplines on our own, perhaps in private, but this is not always so.

Now the next three activities, make no mistake, are going to be public. There is no possible way to engage privately in these next three disciplines. This next one in particular, brotherhood, helps us to bring what may have been private out into the public. Unlike the previous two activities, brotherhood may be something we foster only a couple of times each week, as it requires a different type of effort.

And it's something that is going to challenge us as men because, again, it is complicated!

What's So Complicated About Brotherhood?

This one is difficult to write about because we have developed such a mixed-up idea about male spiritual relationships. Just using all three of these words in combination presents a stumbling block to men–male spiritual relationships? We may not even understand what these words individually mean, let alone together. And please note we are not talking about building relationships for the sake of camaraderie, but in order to help each other stay focused on the one thing that matters–taking action to follow Christ. These relationships are vital, yet men do not pursue them because they are so complicated. A lot of this is going to be uncomfortable at first, but by understanding these next four complications and by joining in the conversation we can overcome the complications and do this together. So let's go.

Here are four complications when it comes to male spiritual relationships:

Trusting Other Men

"My command is this: Love each other as I have loved you."
John 15:12

Men have a lot of baggage regarding male (and female) relationships. We always do. There is not a man alive who has not been hurt or does not have some hang-up about men (and women) that keeps him from trusting. In truth we have all been let down by fathers, pastors, friends, and leaders, and because of this we often have trouble trusting people. Being invited into a deeper relationship with men may trigger our need to address these buried issues and even force us to reckon with them. These injuries we've received may have been a result of gossip, aggression, insincerity, manipulation, abuse, arrogance, or something similar. So we think, why bother? Why subject ourselves to it again? Isn't it better to avoid it altogether?

Having been hurt in the past, we are reluctant to extend trust yet again. This is only the beginning of why male spiritual relationships can be complicated for men.

Most men will go to great lengths to avoid addressing pain unless it is unmistakably pushing itself to the surface. Some men will engage spiritual brotherhood for the first time only after their pain has become unbearable and must be addressed; for instance, they might join a support group for addiction, financial crisis, or divorce. It's much easier to overcome our hurts and hang-ups with relationships when other men share common pain. But it is sad that it takes this much pain to discover all the benefits of spiritual relationships with other men. What we need is a less reactive approach to discovering these benefits. How can we become proactive and pursue them?

We need a much less reactive approach to discovering brotherhood; we need to get proactive.

Jesus indicates above that brotherly love is not only important; it's vital. It is essential for us and essential to our witness. Yet Jesus knows we all have trust issues with loving other brothers. Even saying this feels awkward. The awkwardness stems from our need to be loved, learning to love ourselves properly, discovering that God first loved us, and even learning how to accept love from God and our fellow man. There are so many trust issues that get tangled within a man that requires a lot of effort to untangle. But remember that these issues are solved by engaging in brotherhood–so don't put off brotherhood relationships until after you've sorted out your issues.

I am sure that the twelve disciples who followed Jesus did not always love and trust each other. But over the short time they were with Jesus, they stuck it out together, and Jesus gave them reasons to trust him and each other. The one thing that aided the process was love–a true masculine love that was willing to sacrifice for another brother. Jesus modeled it during his time with them and wanted them to do the same with others. It was a love that transcended hurts and hang-ups and focused on the greater mission at hand.

Corrupt Beliefs About Manhood

> *The eye cannot say to the hand, "I don't need you!" And the head cannot say to the feet, "I don't need you!"* 1 Corinthians 12:21

But there is more. Brotherly love is only the beginning of our complicated issue, for we are rugged, assertive, and independent men.

Men across the world have constructed deeply problematic beliefs and attitudes about manhood. One of them is this sweeping philosophy that men inherently embrace: that we must be rugged, assertive, and independent. This blueprint invented in the mind of men about our masculinity is ingrained into society at large. Travel the world and you'll find the theme is prevalent everywhere.

Messages of rugged, assertive, and independent men come at us in soundbites from just about every angle. Don't believe me? Open up any men's magazine. Listen to advertising for men. Watch any movie marketed to men. Tune into any sports network and watch and listen to what they say and how they act. Messages and images about men being rugged, assertive, and independent are everywhere, and this is the message we believe.

But why is this message for men so prevalent? Because we buy into it; godlike, rugged, assertive independence sells to men. It's everything we want. It's the temptation of the first sin: we want to be like God. I believe it is actually pointless to blame anyone but ourselves on this one. It's nobody's fault but our own. The idea of a rugged, assertive, independent man sells to and feeds our pride, and brotherhood does not. Paul the apostle understood this and communicated a clear counter-cultural message: "We cannot say, 'I don't need you.'"

Paul wonderfully captures our need for each other in this text. He uses a body metaphor to describe a community experience within the church (or in our context, the need for male spiritual brotherhood). That is because we are each essential to a functioning spiritual community. We do not function at our best when we are independent, isolated, autonomous, and alone, but rather in brotherhood.

We do not function at our best when we are independent, isolated, autonomous, and alone, but rather in brotherhood.

In spiritual relationship, we discover benefits that otherwise we don't have. For example, if you have practical needs, a brother can help you. If you are looking for advice or support during a challenging time, brotherhood is the place. Do you need talent or skill you don't have? Invite a Christian brother to help, and he will step in. And most importantly, there is straight-up spiritual provision that can only be found in community. These include things like confession, reconciliation, and forgiveness that are only and exclusively expressed and experienced in relationship. Honestly, brotherhood is the best pro-bono system ever invented; it's where we find everything we need. Where better to learn to deactivate our rugged, assertive independence and activate the spiritual muscle of dependence than with other Christian men?

I get so excited when I see Christian men's groups gathering in cafés, churches, and conference rooms around the world. Nothing could excite me more. When I see them, I think to myself, "These are men fighting against their desire for independence and discovering the benefits of dependence." They are fighting the good fight against the refrain of the independent man who says, "I don't need you."

Speed of Life

> *And let us consider how we may spur one another on toward love and good deeds, not giving up meeting together, as some are in the habit of doing, but encouraging one another—and all the more as you see the Day approaching.* Hebrews 10:24–25

For some men, the speed of life is the most significant complicating factor in their pursuit of brotherhood experiences. We are moving way too fast. And we know it. Actually, life speed can get out of hand for men of all ages, from boys in high school to men who are retired. At times everyone gets too busy. But our busyness is a choice. We make the choice to be overly busy because we prefer to invest our energy and time in other things and put spiritual development and brotherhood on the back burner.

But this is not a new problem invented by modernity.

Notice how the writer above exhorts the Hebrews. He charges them to "not give up meeting together, as some are in the habit of doing." But while giving this challenge, he also recognizes that missing out on brotherhood means we miss out on intended benefits, "spurring one another on toward love, meeting together, and encouraging one another." While busyness may tempt us to "give up" on spiritual brotherhood, what if "not giving up" on spiritual brotherhood actually uncomplicated our busyness?

While busyness may tempt us to "give up" on spiritual brotherhood, what if "not giving up" spiritual brotherhood actually uncomplicated our busyness?

Many men don't realize what they're missing because they have never experienced it. Instead, they pursue what's familiar and become busy, increasing speed, volume, and frequency of activities, but not relationships with other men. We must break this cycle–and do so immediately.

Required Change

> *Do not think of yourself more highly than you ought, but rather think of yourself with sober judgment, in accordance with the faith God has distributed to each of you. For just as each of us has one body with many members, and these members do not all have the same function, so in Christ we, though many, form one body, and each member belongs to all the others.* Romans 12:3–5

Finally, brotherhood requires change. It requires things of us that many have never done before, and therefore we are hesitant to pursue it. More than anything, brotherhood requires us to do something that feels far from masculine: to lay down our issues in the company of other men, and to change. And you thought laying your life down for Christ was a big step!

Some may find this requirement to change to be every bit as daunting. We naturally resist change. And this relational leap is going to challenge most men because they fear everything that spiritual brotherhood demands: transparency, willingness, teachability, exposure, vulnerability, sharing Initially these things appear to be weak, and a waste of time. Many times men who have tasted of spiritual brotherhood sell these demands rather than the benefits of brotherhood when they invite others in. As a result men become intimidated by the prospect of brotherhood; they believe that they're being asked to join a support group where they'll sit around with other men and talk about their feelings and failings. This does happen on occasion, but it's not all that happens. Promoting brotherhood by describing its demands is a hard sell when most men have never experienced or heard of the benefits.

Aside from these four, there are surely more complications. You probably have a list of your own. All the same, we all need to be in relationship. This is not an option; it's a mandate.

And as a brother, allow me to give you a preliminary shove toward the starting line with two ways you can begin to engage in this fundamental.

Preliminary Matters

Take Initiative

Brotherhood requires initiative. Not by someone else: by you.

Evidence shows that men fail to successfully develop meaningful relationships with other men. Men have lots of acquaintances from work, school, life, and even church. We might even have some friends we hang with because we have a few interests in common, like cars, sports, or gaming. But ask a Christian man if he has one (just one!) meaningful spiritual relationship with another man, the answer is usually no.

Some men have gone years and decades without one.

This is insanity. This is a sure plan for failure. By clinging to autonomy just because it's easier, we leave ourselves open to all kinds of issues, problems, and sin. We can't do life this way and be spiritually successful. You may have a believing wife; if so, she's critical. You may even attend church on a regular basis, which is also important. You may even pray and read scripture daily, and yes, and this is also vital. But spiritual brotherhood is an essential part of life and cannot be forgotten. Consider this:

> *Again I saw something meaningless under the sun: There was a man all alone; he had neither son nor brother. There was no end to his toil, yet his eyes were not content with his wealth.* Ecclesiastes 4:7–8

Brotherhood demands one thing at the outset: old-fashioned initiative. No one else can intervene here. It's not going to be planned by your pastor, your wife, or a friend. Only you can reach out to another man. It means you need to assign yourself a task for today. You are probably going to have to pick the phone up and make a call or sit down and write an email. You cannot sit around and wait to be invited; you will need to stretch out some spiritual muscles and start using them (and I will show you how to do it in just a minute). But since I can't do it for you, try remembering this one thing: do something.

Stop clinging to autonomy just because it's easier; take initiative and do something. Be proactive in your spiritual development.

Think Shoulder-to-Shoulder

Now that you are ready to take initiative, and before I give you three practical steps to take, let's try to make taking initiative a little less daunting.

I recognize that if you are doing this on your own, it can be intimidating. If you've never developed a Christian relationship with another man, you may become overwhelmed. The motivational, unempathetic side of me says, "Get over it!" But my supportive side says, "Let's think about it differently."

You should think about initiating brotherhood in one of two ways:

- The shoulder-to-shoulder meet-up—an activity-focused meet-up
- The face-to-face meet-up—a topic-focused meet-up

With either option you are going to have to do a little practical planning. Let's consider what this could look like.

I believe when we are first starting off, it's easier to start with a shoulder-to-shoulder activity, which is far less intimidating. It gives us something to do while we are building a relationship and leaves us with less uncertainty in the schedule. Besides, most guys are a little competitive and energized by doing something that scratches that itch. Just ask some guy to come with you to something that you like to do. Think golf, games, and guns. Activities like skeet shooting, where you are holding a gun and standing shoulder-to-shoulder with another guy can be far less intimidating than sitting face-to-face in a coffee shop.

There are tons of shoulder-to-shoulder activities that you probably already like to do that you could do with other men. Think bowling, darts, racquetball, or pickleball. Think service project, mission trip, or adventure excursion. When we are doing these kinds of activities, I think it's easier for us to give the relationship a test run and figure out if there is a connection of mutual benefit. The fears about vulnerability, emotional sharing, and the appearance of weakness go away because everyone knows what to expect at these outings.

Reduce your fear, take initiative with shoulder-to-shoulder activities that create opportunity for common activity.

But you could always go straight for a face-to-face meet-up over a meal or coffee. Most men are going to be glad you asked, but if you choose this route, it does mean you need to be a little more prepared, because you are going to need things to talk about. You can't just wing it and stare at the other guy. And that's where we are heading next: let's examine about what to talk about during this time.

Feeling brave? Ask for a face-to-face meeting and jump into the deep end of brotherhood.

Build Brotherhood

I have no one else like him. Paul (in reference to Timothy) Philippians 2:20

It's a meet-up; that's all. It's just like any other meeting you've ever had. But in our head, we complicate it because we think spiritual conversations are a lot different. After all, we have never had an intentional spiritual discussion with a guy before, and this other guy might not know what to do, either.

So let me offer you three pointers for structuring the time and the conversation. They play out the same for both types of meet-up: shoulder-to-shoulder and face-to-face.

One | Prepare Four Purposeful Questions

> *Now there was a Pharisee, a man named Nicodemus who was a member of the Jewish ruling council. He came to Jesus at night.* John 3:1–2

When it comes to shoulder-to-shoulder activities, preparation is a little less troublesome. The purpose of the activity determines the flow of the time. However, an intentional spiritual conversation requires a little effort. But only a little.

Here is what I mean. I have walked away from a number of golf events wishing I could have spent more time conversing on important topics with the extraordinary men I was with. Having an intentional conversation about meaningful spiritual content should be one of your primary goals whenever you meet; in some cases even the central activity can take a back seat. Don't let the excitement of the activity hijack the opportunity to be purposeful. You can golf, watch a game, or shoot guns while talking about how to raise God-honoring kids, discussing relational challenges you are facing in your marriage, or acknowledging your anxiety about a looming career change.

If you have not had a purposeful conversation before while doing a shoulder-to-shoulder activity, then just tell your friend at the outset that you'd like to pick his brain about a couple of topics during the activity or afterward. It's not weird to do this. Many a business deal is struck while swinging sticks on a golf course. This just happens to be a spiritual deal with spiritual implications. Just make sure to be clear about the purpose for the invite so your friend doesn't feel ambushed. (I have included some inviting language below to help you out.)

Spiritual brothers ask purposeful questions of each other.

If you are skipping the shoulder-to-shoulder activity and going straight for a face-to-face meet-up, then you need to determine the purpose up front.

Since you'll be primarily (if not exclusively) conversing, there won't be many distractions aside from food or beverages.

The conversational key to either type of meeting is simply this: your topic determines your purpose. The central topic of discussion is the purpose of the meeting. Before I extend an invitation to a Christian brother for a meet-up, first I determine four questions I want to ask, and from these questions comes the purpose. These questions can help you to determine the type of man you need to connect with. For example, if you need business advice, meet a Christian businessman. Need marital advice, meet with a Christian man who been through your challenges. Need kid advice, talk to a Christian father who has three or more children. I think you get it; it's pretty intuitive, but we over-complicate these things. It's just a meet-up with a spiritual focus.

Now you need to go prepare your questions.

If you need some inviting starter language, here are some lines that might help:

The general meet-up:

- I want to pick your brain on a couple of subjects.
- I am facing a challenge, and I want to get your opinion.
- I see you're great at [fill in the blank] and I want to understand how you do it.

The "I'm a new Christian" meet-up:

- I am new to a relationship with Christ, and I'm looking for some wisdom on some topics.
- I am challenging myself to connect with other Christian men this year.
- I am looking for some spiritual guidance and thought you might be able to help.

Career advice meet-up:

- I am facing some challenges at work, and I want to pick your brain.

- I am considering a career change and want to know how you made your transition.
- I am looking to network with some Christian men.

The tune-up meet-up:
- I am looking for one to two guys to connect with on a weekly basis.
- I am looking for practical advice on [insert topic]; would you be willing to grab some coffee?

The serious meet-up:
- I've been praying about an issue, and I'm not sure what to do. I thought you could help.
- I was recently laid off and need some career direction.
- I am facing a series of challenging events and need some guidance and prayer.
- I heard you have faced similar challenges; can you show me how you overcame?

Get One Tip

> *And let us consider how we may spur one another on toward love and good deeds, not giving up meeting together, as some are in the habit of doing, but encouraging one another—and all the more as you see the Day approaching.* Hebrews 10:24–25

Next, what's the goal of the meet-up?

This too is simple and often overlooked. In the context of Christian brotherhood, we are always seeking to become more like Christ and trying to encourage each other toward that end. That's the bottom line. I believe the easiest way to do this is one tip at a time.

In every relationship, I am looking to leave every meet-up having received something that pays out dividends in my life or, conversely, having left something for my brother that will pay out dividends to him.

I want to be better for having met with my brothers, and they with me. Therefore, during our meeting I am looking for an encouraging slant I hadn't considered before, a new revelation, or an insight into one of our issues. When we're engaging in intentional conversation, we are going to discover something new about ourselves–at least I almost always do. In some cases, we may learn many things. We are mining for the gold in this relationship. I call it looking for a tip.

Spiritual brothers leave better than they came–making an investment in each other.

If you are struggling to know what kind of tip you may need, dig into those 5-F categories (faith, family, fitness, finance, and friendships) and identify some tips you need for personal improvement. Then go back to the previous step and consider if the questions lead to this end.

The best practice is to restate your new insights, the tip you gained, to the man that you're meeting with before you leave. In doing this, you are both thanking him and letting him know that the time impacted you. You should see a man's face when you do this; he lights up almost every time.

So remember: prepare four questions and get one tip.

Add in One Spiritual Element

Therefore encourage one another and build each other up, just as in fact you are doing. Thessalonians 5:11

Lastly, you need to add in a spiritual element to every Christian meet-up. It's key to do this early and often. If you can establish this pattern from the first meeting, this will serve as a bit of an icebreaker for future spiritual development. Some men are going to be challenged on this one since they have never taken those previous two fundamentals, prayer and scripture, public before. Here is a little progression over three meetings that I would use if you feel unsure of where to lead things.

- Meet-up #1: Ask at the end how you can pray for him that week.
- Meet-up #2: Ask permission to pray before the meeting; then pray out loud and keep it short.
- Meet-up #3: Share about some scripture you've been reading and get his thoughts; then engage in prayer as you did in the second meet-up.

It's better to introduce spiritual activity earlier than later in the relationship, because if you put it off for too long, you won't ever get around to doing it. Pierce through the awkwardness of spiritual openness; lean into it.

Spiritual brothers include spiritual elements into the meet-ups.

Remember to prepare four questions, get one tip, and add in one spiritual element. I call this the 411 on Brotherhood so that it's easy to remember.

As a final word of encouragement you may not succeed in developing a brotherhood relationship with a single meet-up, and that's okay. Any number of factors can cause a failed connection, many of which are totally out of your control. What is important is that you take initiative, develop a plan, and leave the results up to God. If it doesn't work, consider what was off in the connection, and then go find another guy who fits what you are looking for. You don't have to establish a connection with one guy forever if the mutual relationship only has a seasonal benefit for you both.

Remember, Jesus didn't hang with his twelve guys forever. You need not be exclusive in every relationship, but neither should you quickly discard relationships. In thc end, the key is to not give up. Brotherhood is vital to your spiritual development, and the benefits are incredible.

Reflection & Discussion Questions

1. Why are friendships important to all men?
2. How is spiritual brotherhood different from other friendships?
3. How could a spiritual brother make you a better husband, father, friend, and coworker?
4. What type of spiritual brother do you currently need in your life?
5. Are you willing to let go of other priorities (or even relationships) to develop a solid relationship with another Christian brother?

Call To Action

The following steps are your call to action in the area of brotherhood.

1 | Preliminary Matters:

- **Take Initiative:** make the decision to own the needed action to build a relationship with another man. Name a Christian brother that you need to be spending time with.
- **Think Shoulder-to-Shoulder:** invite the person above along for an activity or meet-up. Decide your activity and then call, text, or email him.

2 | Build Brotherhood:

- **Prepare 4 Questions:** you would like to ask. What are your questions?
- **Get 1 Tip:** that you can take away from the time together–and then thank him. Is there a tip you want to get?
- **Add in 1 Spiritual Element:** of any kind. Decide in advance to do this: it could be as simple as a prayer or thought from your reading in scripture. What's the element you want to include?

If you want help stepping through this consider following along with me on the **35-Day Challenge** that pairs with this book. Check it out online at www.beresolute.org/called-to-act.

11

Accountability

Let's go back to the Parable of the Sower for just a moment. I want to look back at something with you. The point of the parable is this: a man's receptivity of God's Word matters. We also discovered that a man's level of receptivity determines the produce of his life. It's either nothing or it's something–and when it's something it's incredible. Remember: we are talking about spiritual receptivity to truth–and not just any truth, but *God's* truth.

This means that spiritual outcomes correspond in some way to our spiritual receptivity. On our human level we must exert some effort in being receptive. On a spiritual level God exerts effort; this is called grace, love, mercy, and forgiveness. And in harmony we accomplish unthinkable, impossible, and miraculous things. What's required of you to become a man called to act? Only one thing: receptivity. That's it. Receptivity is a big thing because it leads to change in everything, but nothing else will equip us for action.

"Pay attention to yourselves!" Luke 17:3a

It's paying attention. That's it.

Who wouldn't want to be around an attentive and receptive man? They are more willing, curious, and free. They are also less dogmatic, rigid, and stuck. They are more willing to try new experiences and experiment with new ways of doing things. And while excessive openness can be ineffective and aimless in the human experience, this is not so in our relationship with Christ. For in our relationship, there is one who always changes–*us*–and one who does not–*Christ.*

In our relationship, there is one who always changes—us—
and one who does not—Christ.

Now let's look at the full passage from Luke 17:3. The second half of the verse is a bit of a shocker, but read it for all the benefits.

> *Pay attention to yourselves! If your brother or sister sins against you, rebuke them; and if they repent, forgive them.* Luke 17:3

If we can look beyond the tough language we will see all the beauty of accountability that most men miss. Accountability helps us to pay attention and become receptive. It brings us into relationship. It preserves relationships. It aids us in our war with sin. It builds courage in a man during challenging times. It can lead to repentance and forgiveness. It promotes healing and character in men. But the real benefit we tend to overlook is the *awareness* it provides. Accountability helps us to *"pay attention to ourselves"* in a manner we cannot achieve alone.

Our impulse is to *man-up* (I strongly dislike this language, by the way) with our rugged, assertive independence and do life alone. Instead we need to *brother-up* and welcome accountability on the journey of becoming the man God intended us to be. And here is why.

It's Inevitable

> *"But I tell you that everyone will have to give account on the day of judgment for every empty word they have spoken."* Matthew 12:36

I don't know whether you've discovered this yet, but accountability is inevitable. It's one of those life principles you cannot avoid. You will pay now or pay later. You can't dodge accountability, even though many men think they can. Eventually all men will stand before the throne of God and give account. This is the ultimate pay-later principle. So as men, why not be more proactive and less reactive? Let's pay now with a little spiritual discipline, some uneasy faith sharing, and the loss of toxic friendships—so we don't have to pay later. Let's endure the shame today of being called out, allowing our sin to be exposed, and then let's turn to God in daily repentance. Why not embrace being called out by a wife or a Christian friend rather than have a crowd expose your flaws? Why not rather be corrected by a senior executive and endure a change than be fired from a job? Why not endure a talk-down by a drill sergeant than endure humiliation and loss in battle? I don't know about you, but a little temporary pain sounds better than the long-term loss and embarrassment. It's that old pay-now-or-pay-later principle. As Jesus said in the passage above, if we don't steer our choices in a godly direction, there's always a penalty to be paid. So why not invite Christians we trust to help us stay on course?

> *Nothing in all creation is hidden from God's sight. Everything is uncovered and laid bare before the eyes of him to whom we must give account.* Hebrews 4:13

God is all about accountability. For him to be truthful (and in fact he *is* the truth) he will always be the champion of great accountability. From the first pages of the Bible to the last, he calls all men to account for what they have done. So if you think you can avoid accountability, you are wrong. The real choice is ours: we can either pay now or pay later. We can be proactive in pursuing accountability or be reactive and forced to give account. We can submit to discipline now or be disciplined later.

Preliminary Matters

If you have worked in a high-accountability environment, you know that accountability works. I have a few friends that work in highly managed occupations whose daily actions are monitored carefully by numerous people. These friends work in settings that protect and care for human life. And while this sounds burdensome, they welcome, invite, and want accountability. More eyes and better accountability ensure better outcomes in the end.

In a spiritual context, we must look for accountability around our action and motivations, and it can feel daunting. Rather than talk about each and every reason we resist accountability with other men, here is a quick list; I am sure you could add a few of your own.

- We enjoy our privacy.
- We've had bad experiences with sharing private details with others.
- We've don't know how to do it.
- We're afraid of being exposed.
- We're fiercely independent.
- We don't want to look weak.
- We don't really want to change.
- We believe we are only accountable to God.

I have heard every one of these excuses from men, and I'm guilty of having said a few on this list earlier in my life. But all of our hesitations boil down to one big issue when it comes to accountability for men. It's not an issue with the purpose, process, or the people. It's an issue with us. We simply harbor too many bad beliefs and attitudes about Christian accountability.

Ditch the Bad Beliefs and Attitudes

> *"You hypocrite, first take the plank out of your own eye, and then you will see clearly to remove the speck from your brother's eye."*
> Matthew 7:5

Let's be really honest about this. Men have a lot of misinformed beliefs and a really hostile attitude when it comes to spiritual accountability. I have found that men have all kinds of baggage buried deep down on this one.

Some of us have been burned by other Christians who manipulated us; and often we simply like life as it is. Let's admit it: we can be stubborn. Besides, *"plucking logs out of our eyeballs"* does not sound like fun; frankly, it sounds severe. We'd be better off without the log sticking out, but in the end, it's an elective surgery, right? I think you would agree, it's pretty obvious why men aren't lining up, cheering, and rubbing their hands to get down and dirty in some good old-fashioned accountability.

What's so ironic is that we actually love accountability when it's exerted on other people. We love it when that guy who cut us off in traffic gets pulled over a mile up the road (and whenever it doesn't play out that way, we enjoy imagining that outcome). When our team is playing a fierce opponent, we love it when a player we despise gets called for a penalty, gets sent to the bench, and has to watch our team steal the win. We love it when that deceitful, manipulative, narcissistic leader finally gets busted. We feel good when it happens, justified, and satisfied in some strange way. So deep down we really love accountability. We just would rather not experience it ourselves.

This love-hate relationship results in twisted beliefs and attitudes that stem from a complete misunderstanding of accountability. Most of the time when men hear the word accountability in Christian circles, they hear about it in conjunction with sin and sexual compulsions. In recent years, books and resources for men in sexual addiction have become more abundant than ever. The core messaging presented is that accountability offers a way out. Mind you, this isn't wrong. Some type of accountability is absolutely needed in situations where men are stuck in repetitive sin, but that's not the full picture of what accountability can be or why we need to embrace it.

I believe accountability can be proactive and positive. Think of the accountability you see exhibited between a great coach and a great player. There are a number of these great coach-to-player relationships in just about any sport, so think of one of them. What kinds of things is this coach doing to hold his player accountable? He is training, preparing, leading, building up, and on some occasions tearing down. But he is not constantly coming at this player with reactive and negative accountability. Instead, the coach works to find an approach that's right for the man in his charge, with the goal of building him into a better player, better leader, and better man.

Now let's apply this to spiritual accountability for men. The intent of accountability should be to make us better men, father, husbands, and leaders. It's proactive and positive, not exclusively used to keep us from sin, but rather to teach, rebuke, correct, and train us to become the man God wants us to be.

So what does positive, proactive Christian accountability look like? Can it be built around me learning to accept more of God's grace, forgiveness, love, and mercy during the week? Can it be built around conversations that encourage me to pray, read scripture, build brotherhood, and engage in ministry with greater effectiveness? Can it be about actionable outcomes that I need to work on with my wife, kids, friends, and peers at work? Isn't this what we want? It's definitely what we need. We just need to get past the rub of the bad beliefs and attitudes.

As iron sharpens iron, so one person sharpens another. Proverbs 27:17

This one verse is an iconic men's ministry verse. But men need to learn to move past memorization and come to love the process described by this verse: when iron sharpens iron, a wheel is grinding, sparks are flying, and the room is filled with the shriek of an iron-on-iron scuffling rub. The sounds and sensations of this grind can be painful, but it's what we must endure to achieve a sharpened instrument. I believe the first dull spots we men need to grind away are all our bad beliefs and bad attitudes. And remember, if you don't push through the discomfort of this moment, you'll end up doing nothing–and inactive iron rusts.

So we need to ditch all these bad beliefs and attitudes. Go ahead and write them down for your own personal awareness. Start including them in your prayer time as part of a confession to yourself and to God. For example, you could say something like this:

- *God, I have lived isolated for too long.*
- *God, I have had a suspicious attitude about Christian men in general.*
- *God, I am scared of being exposed; I have sin in my life I am not ready to confess to others.*

- *God, I feel like I have made too many mistakes.*
- *God, I don't feel accepted by the men of my church.*
- *God, I am scared of change.*
- *God, I have been hurt by accountability in the past.*
- *God, I am scared of looking weak by going to that group.*

This may sound a little heavy at this point, but we need to get past all this garbage and discover the joy of a new perspective.

> *Consider it pure joy, my brothers and sisters, whenever you face trials of many kinds, because you know that the testing of your faith produces perseverance. Let perseverance finish its work so that you may be mature and complete, not lacking in anything.* James 1:2–4

Instead of focusing on all these bad things, we need to embrace the attitude of joy. We need to more quickly submit to the test that produces endurance so that we can be complete as a man.

I want to show you another way of doing accountability that will take a lot of your concerns off the table. It might even make it joyful and inviting for you. Let's focus on positive and proactive activities that will perhaps make it different from other experiences you have had. Are you ready to ditch those old bad attitudes and beliefs once and for all?

Let's talk about two preliminary items that must be addressed before we begin.

Determine One Area that You Want to Improve

> *Don't let anyone look down on you because you are young, but set an example for the believers in speech, in conduct, in love, in faith and in purity.* 1 Timothy 4:12

As we get started in accountability, we need to set some kind of goal. In the verse above, Paul is giving his protégé Timothy some goals to consider in the behavior, character, and virtue departments. It's clear that Paul knows Timothy well and wants to help him along. But Timothy must embrace this call to action for himself. Timothy must determine to do it on his own. Paul cannot make him do it.

To get started, all you need to do is determine one goal for your personal and spiritual growth from among the 5-F categories: *faith*, *family*, *finance*, *fitness*, and *friendships*. Surely you could identify one goal from each category, but that's not a great idea. You'd have to dilute your focus, which would likely cause you to either forget some of your goals or stumble and fail across the board. Set yourself up for early success: select just one goal for a number of weeks and scale up as you go.

We live in a world overloaded with information so we must prioritize and focus in order to succeed. This is especially true for us as men. In order to accomplish a meaningful goal, we need to fight back at attempting to do too much at once. With so many other competing priorities, it's easy for meaningful goals to become forgotten. So just make one goal. You'll find it easy to remember, you'll more easily find help and support, and you'll stay flexible, able to spend as much time and energy as you need to accomplish that one goal. Trust me on this one.

Take a moment and write down your goal here in 3–5 words:

Now you have one more preliminary thing to do with this same goal.

Describe the Outcome of the Goal

> *And after you have suffered a little while, the God of all grace, who has called you to his eternal glory in Christ, will himself restore, confirm, strengthen, and establish you.* 1 Peter 5:10

You'll notice that Peter understands there is purpose in every kind of suffering. We just don't always see it in the moment. There is also pain that comes from suffering. But the best part of proactive and positive accountability is that we get to determine the goal and have a purpose for enduring the pain.

The best part of proactive and positive accountability is that we get to determine the goal and have a purpose for enduring the pain.

The next important step is to take your one goal and imagine how your life would be different if you accomplished it. I want you to imagine how your life would be *"restored, confirmed, strengthened, and established"* as Peter talks about above. How would your life be different if you were successful in this one area? You need to write it down. Consider how your success would affect the people around you. Consider how your success would change your thoughts, attitudes, and actions. Consider what the new you would look like.

Take a moment and write here a 2 or 3-sentence description of the man you would be.

These two preliminary steps are critical; without them you cannot move forward and effectively engage in accountability.

D.O. Accountability

So now it's time to untangle every belief and attitude you have about accountability by learning a better approach. This is how you should *D.O. it.* (Notice the acronym there.)

Declare It

> *Therefore confess your sins to each other and pray for each other so that you may be healed. The prayer of a righteous person is powerful and effective.* James 5:16

It's time to go public with what you have determined and described above. Since you already know what you want to accomplish, this makes taking the next step easy. All you have to do is *declare it.*

Notice what James said above. He uses the word *confession,* which means *to agree with, acknowledge, or declare.* And notice its obvious benefits.

Don't wait to go public and declare. Share your intent with someone. Given the challenge of the last chapter, you could declare this to the brother you want to connect with, which is a great idea. You could declare it to a spouse, another great idea. Want to be really bold? Declare it on social media. But get it out there.

Declare it: go public with your accountability goal and outcome.

There are two reasons to do this. First, when you declare this publicly, you are pledging yourself to action. If you end up doing nothing, it'll reflect poorly on you in a way that wouldn't have happened if you'd kept your goal to yourself. This desire to demonstrate the integrity of your word can be a powerful motivating factor. Second, a declaration helps others to help you. James is spot on with this. When people know what you are trying to do, they can also pray for the outcome you seek–it's powerful and effective! So if you want results, *declare it.*

And then there is only one step left.

Own It

> *Each one should test their own actions. Then they can take pride in themselves alone, without comparing themselves to someone else, for each one should carry their own load.* Galatians 6:4–5

Not only do you need to declare your need to change, but you need to *own it.* It's your responsibility.

I think accountability gets complicated because we tend to expect somebody else to provide the muscle and then pull and drag us forward. Please note: other men are rarely (and I mean *rarely*) going to own the check-in process with you. Most of the time they will forget, unless they are extremely disciplined. For most men, accountability looks more like a one-time confession to an accountability partner or even a group of men. We'll include an invitation for other men to hold us accountable, but the check-in part of the process never happens. Surprised? Probably not.

Here's the game changer: Recognize it's your job to lead and direct this process. You determine the goal, you describe the outcome, you declare your intent, and then you own responsibility for the check in; it's your initiative all the way through to the end. It's not someone else's responsibility to hold you accountable; it's yours. You are responsible to initiate conversations in which you tell the truth about what's going on in your growth process. Accountability only works when you pursue it. Nobody can corner you into the sort of honesty that leads to change. You must be willing to set a goal, willing to change, willing to get help, and willing to invite check-in.

Own it. It's your job to lead and direct the process not someone else's.

Instead of waiting for someone else to check in with you, make a plan in advance about when you can share your progress. I would start by checking in once per week for three-week total. You could check in through text or phone call, or you can meet face to face. During these check-ins, discuss your progress toward your goal by addressing these three topics:

- What you need to **start** doing.
- What you need to **stop** doing.
- What you need to **continue** doing.

It's pretty simple, so don't over-complicate it. Eventually you will discover significant progress, or you might need to adjust the goal slightly given what you are learning about yourself and your situation.

Now it's your turn. You've been presented with a new approach to doing accountability. It's super positive and proactive. The only question is: *will you act?*

Reflection & Discussion Questions

1. What's your present attitude toward spiritual accountability?
2. Why do we not see more proactive accountability among men in spiritual relationships?
3. On a scale of 1 to 10, how receptive are you to spiritual accountability in your life?
4. What would make spiritual accountability more inviting for you?

Call to Action

The following steps are your call to action in the area of accountability. Take a few minutes to address the preliminary issues and then do them.

1 | Preliminary Matters:

- **Ditch:** the bad beliefs you have about accountability. Write one down and confess it.
- **Determine:** one area where you would like to improve spiritually. Write it down.

- **Describe:** the outcome of the goal you determined above. Write it out.

2 | D.O. Accountability:

- **Declare It:** *Go public with you goal. Who will you share this with?*
- **Own It:** *Own the process for the coming weeks and circle back with the person you declared it to. How will you circle back with this person?*

If you want help stepping through accountability, consider following along with me on the **35-Day Challenge** that pairs with this book. I will guide you step-by-step using the principles above. Check it out online at www.beresolute.org/called-to-act.

12

Ministry

This brings us to the last of the five fundamental disciplines and the most motivating for us as men. We were designed to act, to get things done, to produce, and to find creative ways to use the restless energy God gave us. We were created with a purpose, and that purpose is to join God in his work, to act as his representative wherever you go and in whatever you do.

Now think about that for a second. What incredible responsibility!

What's Complicated About Ministry

There are a number of things that make ministry complicated for men. These factors are top on the list.

The Complication of My Design

You were not made by mistake. God designed men purposefully, and so one of the challenges of our journey is making sense of our design. As men we have this insatiable drive to live purposeful lives. But when we begin our spiritual journey, it feels like our life gets turned upside down—or maybe it's better said, right side up. The former purposes we established for ourselves must be abandoned as we seek to discover God's purpose for us. While this process is exciting, new, and full of adventure, it can be more than a little challenging. Just consider for a moment what Paul says:

> *For we are God's handiwork, created in Christ Jesus to do good works, which God prepared in advance for us to do.* Ephesians 2:10

"We are God's handiwork." The image is striking. Put another way, we are individually hand-made by the Creator. Each of us is a unique and one-of-a-kind work of God. And while we have days when we do not fully understand our purpose, this doesn't change the reality of our nature: God crafted us purposefully. He made you distinct from others by creating your particular mix of talents, abilities, and gifts.

Paul also states that we were "created in Christ Jesus to do good works." His point is simple. God designed you purposefully, but also for a purpose. When God hand-crafted you, he did so with an intended outcome. You can be confident of this. Your design–made manifest through your talents, gifts, and abilities–is direct evidence of your purpose: to channel everything you are into good works. These good works to which God has called us are our ministry.

God designed you purposefully, but also for a purpose—to do good works.

Paul goes even a step further and says that God has "prepared" this job for us "in advance." This is affirming and powerful stuff; we often look forward to how God might help us in the future, but let's remember to stop and think about all the ways God has directed our path to this pivotal moment.

Although we may be confident in the knowledge that we have a purpose, identifying that purpose can still be complicated. The problem here isn't reluctance to discover the plan God has prepared us for; we'd love to live in the middle of God's intended purpose. But the crucial details of how God wants us to live out that purpose often appear distant and impossible to discern.

We will uncomplicate this learning process, but for now, don't be dismayed: God wants you to discover and steward the good works, the ministry he has called you to do.

The Complication of My Fit in the Church

> *Just as a body, though one, has many parts, but all its many parts form one body, so it is with Christ.*
> *The eye cannot say to the hand, "I don't need you!" And the head cannot say to the feet, "I don't need you!" On the contrary, those parts of the body that seem to be weaker are indispensable, and the parts that we think are less honorable we treat with special honor. And the parts that are unpresentable are treated with special modesty, while our presentable parts need no special treatment. But God has put the body together, giving greater honor to the parts that lacked it, so that there should be no division in the body, but that its parts should have equal concern for each other. If one part suffers, every part suffers with it; if one part is honored, every part rejoices with it. Now you are the body of Christ, and each one of you is a part of it.*
> 1 Corinthians 12:12, 21–27

Men are deeply exasperated with the church in our time. They share with me their complaints, challenges, and concerns. It is clear that they are not complaining because they dislike the church, but because they love the church. They want to see the church perform at its very best. They want to connect with a congregation, support it, bring others to it, and especially find their purposeful fit within it.

We must first recognize that the church is essential both to the world and to each of us as believers. Paul was clear about this when he wrote to the Corinthian church. Since the church is essential, must conclude that we cannot just punt on being a church; we must worship together and actively participate in ministry together.

But even with the conviction that we ought to belong to a congregation, discovering our fit within the church remains just as complicated as learning our overall purpose. There are times we just don't see how we fit into the picture. This struggle to connect is especially pronounced when you first join a new congregation. You may feel as though everyone has a place and a role except for you. Or maybe your church has the opposite problem, and nobody can agree on who ought to lead or participate in the various groups and ministries. As discouraged as we may feel, Paul reminds us that the early church had the same problem that we have, even from the very start and in some of the first churches. This was the very issue that prompted Paul's letter to the Corinthian church.

Men were frustrated with the church even in its prototype stage. But Paul explicitly says we cannot punt on the church or on our individual engagement in the church. Even when we struggle to understand our fit within the church, we must struggle through the complication. And why? Because the body will limp (ineffectively) along without you. The body needs you, just as it needs others. But don't miss this: you need them, too. You must not forget that you need to be supported by the talents, abilities, and gifts of others, just as they need to lean on yours. Remember, your talents, abilities, and gifts were not given to you for your own benefit, they are for good works. Freely invest them in others within your church as you prepare to do even greater good works together. If you punt on church, then yes, the congregation is going to miss out on you, but you are going to miss out on them as well. Everyone suffers.

Everyone suffers when we punt on the church.

I am also aware that many of us may resist the idea of joining any church, not because of a stubborn individualistic streak, but due to previous painful experiences. Trust me, I get it. And I agree, the church is flawed, but that should surprise no one, because every church is made up of fallen men just like you and me. Yet the church is still God's vehicle of choice for showing his love to the world. Besides, Jesus loves his church. He loves it a lot. Therefore, we must struggle through this complication, even as we are trying to find our fit in the church. And it may take years for us to find it. You might even have to endure staffing issues, small-group problems, grotesque sins, and even theological issues, but the body will ultimately function better if we can push through the complicating issues.

The Complication of Self-disqualification

> *Now if the foot should say, "Because I am not a hand, I do not belong to the body," it would not for that reason stop being part of the body. And if the ear should say, "Because I am not an eye, I do not belong to the body," it would not for that reason stop being part of the body. If the whole body were an eye, where would the sense of hearing be? If the whole body were an ear, where would the sense of smell be? But in fact God has placed the parts in the body, every one of them, just as he wanted them to be. If they were all one part, where would the body be? As it is, there are many parts, but one body.* 1 Corinthians 12:15–20

Here's a big issue for men: self-disqualification.

Men often think they are not good enough, not educated enough, not knowledgeable enough. Too immature, too young, too old, or too used up. Men think their inability to teach, their weaknesses as a leader, or their lack of a title means that they can't participate in God's kingdom in a meaningful way. Men will always feel they need a little more experience, more permission, and more support. And these voices of negative self-talk cause a leadership implosion in the church as its men disengage.

Honestly, we need to stop this.

If the Holy Spirit lives within you, this is all the qualification you need. The voice of self-disqualification is not of God; it contradicts God, who has already given you your purpose and equipped you to carry it out.

> *When they saw the courage of Peter and John and realized that they were unschooled, ordinary men, they were astonished and they took note that these men had been with Jesus.* Acts 4:13

Check out Peter and John. I bet they heard the voice of self-disqualification. Even the crowd deemed them under-qualified. But empowered by God, their "unschooled" approach illuminated their action, and observers "saw their courage." This is evidence that God can do anything with any man. Even the average man. When a man acts courageously against the voice of self-disqualification, God can do more than any man can do on his own. As man acts in obedience, God does something astonishing.

When a man acts courageously against the voice of self-disqualification, God can do more than any man can do on his own.

We must keep in mind that ministry work follows a different set of rules than what we're used to. In most other vocational fields, you need a vast education, a lot of preparation, and even permission (i.e., certification or a license). Ministry does not play by these same rules. While we do educate ourselves in God's Word, prepare our hearts in prayer, and even ordain ministers, this is all secondary to simply taking action in faith. God doesn't need our knowledge or experience but rather our faithful obedience. Through this action, God does the work. The things he does through us are greater than anything we could do through our own ability. While we can find personal enrichment in the pursuit of education, training, and affirmation, these have no bearing on what God is able to do through us. He is merely looking for men to hear and act, so that he can get to work.

The one who calls you is faithful, and he will do it.
1 Thessalonians 5:24

So never let education, preparation, or permission hold you back. Excessive focus on these can amplify the voice of self-disqualification.

Here is a great Old Testament moment that illustrates this very point. King David is handing the leadership baton off to his son Solomon, who is soon to be king. David was for many reasons qualified to conquer the land, but God had specifically forbidden him from building a Temple. However, David did not allow this one prohibition to stop him from laying the groundwork. Historical records show that David gathered every possible resource the Temple's construction would require. He honored God's instruction and stopped short of construction itself while doing everything he was qualified to do. He didn't sit the corner and sob because he was disqualified from one specific act; instead he did everything possible to support the process. He gathered every necessary ounce of gold and silver, every stone, and every plank of wood. He hired the workers. He established the leadership infrastructure. He developed the plans and their scope and sequence, and all with God's help. Once everything was in order, David handed it to his son. And here is what David said to Solomon:

> *David also said to Solomon his son, "Be strong and courageous, and do the work. Do not be afraid or discouraged, for the Lord God, my God, is with you."* 1 Chronicles 28:20

All that was required for Solomon was faithful courage, nothing more. Talk about succession planning. Everything had been done for him by his father. And here David seeks to mute Solomon's voice of self-disqualification, which was the only thing able to keep him from accomplishing the task.

In the same way, our Father has gathered up endless resources. Our Father has done all the groundwork. He's defeated sin. He's given us the Spirit; the greatest force on planet Earth dwells within us. He extends limitless resources of grace, mercy, forgiveness, and love. He has done all this, and yet we often listen to the voice of self-disqualification, hesitate, and remain in a perpetual stall when all we need is a little courage.

God is ready to do things in and through you right now. Don't allow guilt, shame, and fear to paralyze you. You may feel you have no talents, abilities, and gifts to speak of, but this is a misperception. If you have been born of Christ, you are ready and endowed with power. Self-disqualifying thoughts and beliefs are your only true obstacle; God can help you conquer everything else. As soon as you hurdle this obstacle and get moving, you'll discover this fact–God calls men and equips them along the way. Self-disqualification is all that can keep great men like you and I from achieving greatness. God can help us to defeat any adversary–but he won't make us act.

> *But to those whom God has called, both Jews and Greeks, Christ [is] the power of God and the wisdom of God. For the foolishness of God is wiser than human wisdom, and the weakness of God is stronger than human strength.* 1 Corinthians 1:24–25

You're a Man Repurposed

> *And he gave the apostles, the prophets, the evangelists, the shepherds and teachers, to equip the saints for the work of ministry, for building up the body of Christ, until we all attain to the unity of the faith and of the knowledge of the Son of God, to mature manhood, to the measure of the stature of the fullness of Christ.* Ephesians 4:11–13

As we wrestle to understand our design, our fit within the body of Christ, and the nature of our qualifications, we have to start thinking properly about self and ministry. At its core, ministry is the action of a godly man.

Ministry is our way of life. Few of us think of ministry so broadly because we tend to disassociate our everyday life from our Christian experience. We love the idea of a Savior (who saves us from sin and death), but this whole idea of having a Lord (the leader of our life) is harder to accept. Lordship suggests a lot of new changes to a man's life; it demands that we surrender to a new way and understanding of life. Our post-Lord life should not be what it was pre-Lord.

I understand why men disassociate their "normal" life from their call to ministry. First, their frame of reference includes a pastor, or pastoral staff paid to lead, teach, direct, and care for people. As a result, men think ministry is reserved for those who are paid to do it. Most men assume paid, professional ministry is the only way to do ministry, failing to recognize the universal call to ministry of all believers. Second, some men further conclude that since they are serving in a non-ministry related career, ministry will have to wait until after they get done with their career. For now, they will just do life as usual; they will care and provide for themselves and their family financially and worry about ministry concerns later. But this is a false choice. You can have a non-ministry related career for your whole life without waiting to obey God's call to ministry.

Ministry is not something we can only do as a profession, nor can it wait until later in life, nor is it optional. Ministry is the way that every faithful Christian man carries out his life. And this means we need to see the entirety of our way of life as ministry.

Take a look at Paul. He wrote most of the New Testament. His credentials are incredible:

> *Though I myself have reasons for such confidence. If someone else thinks they have reasons to put confidence in the flesh, I have more: circumcised on the eighth day, of the people of Israel, of the tribe of Benjamin, a Hebrew of Hebrews; in regard to the law, a Pharisee; as for zeal, persecuting the church; as for righteousness based on the law, faultless.* Philippians 3:4–6

Paul had tremendous real-world experience, even more than what is mentioned here. God used Paul's training, background, legal experience, influence, heritage, political influence, and his writing and speaking ability to transform Paul into a worldwide force for ministry in the most powerful empire of his day—the Roman Empire. Paul is an interesting example of the everyday man because most of his talents, abilities, and gifts were being prepared and polished before he ever became a Christian. That's right: Paul continued to use the same talents, abilities, and gifts that he always had, but following his conversion God repurposed them for kingdom influence.

The book of Romans in the New Testament is a perfect example of this. This letter, written by Paul, is evidence of his legal skill, leadership influence, political savvy, religious upbringing, and even his knowledge of

Greek and Roman philosophies. Paul wrote this shining legal argument for the faith to followers in Rome. It's one of the greatest arguments of all time. From this we can see that God had a plan for Paul, and that Paul's talents, abilities, and gifts had been repurposed for influence in a new way. Paul understood that it was only by God's mercy and grace that this was possible.

> *I thank Christ Jesus our Lord, who has given me strength, that he considered me trustworthy, appointing me to his service. Even though I was once a blasphemer and a persecutor and a violent man, I was shown mercy because I acted in ignorance and unbelief. The grace of our Lord was poured out on me abundantly, along with the faith and love that are in Christ Jesus.* 1 Timothy 1:12–14

I cannot think of a man more initially disqualified–and then, post-Christ, qualified and repurposed–than Paul. But guess what? He's just like you and me and every other man. As a result of God's mercy and grace Paul was a man repurposed. Those seemingly natural talents, abilities, and gifts were leveraged for kingdom purposes. Formerly Paul used them for his own purposes and his own glory, but now they were being used for God's purposes and God's glory.

Formerly they were used for Paul's purposes and his glory, and now they were being used for God's purposes and God's glory.

Jesus knew what he was doing with Paul. Just listen to Ananias's concern as Jesus asked him to go and heal Paul (then known as Saul).

> *"Lord," Ananias answered, "I have heard many reports about this man and all the harm he has done to your holy people in Jerusalem. And he has come here with authority from the chief priests to arrest all who call on your name."*

But the Lord said to Ananias, "Go! This man is my chosen instrument to proclaim my name to the Gentiles and their kings and to the people of Israel. I will show him how much he must suffer for my name."
Acts 9:13–16

As men called to ministry under the lordship of Jesus Christ, we need to have the same perspective. You are a man who God has intentionally repurposed. You have been saved by the mercy and grace of God. God has chosen you for his purposes. Despite a few complications that cause us hesitation, Jesus sees us as regenerated men positioned for impact. No longer shall we serve our own purposes, but God's.

So how do we do this?

Activate Ministry

We have concluded that scripture is clear: we are designed by God, therefore designed on purpose and given a purpose along with abilities, talents, and gifts to be repurposed. You have unique gifts at your disposal. Each man does. We were given them by God, and it appears even prior to our birth he was knitting something together in us. God intentionally crafted and made each of us, giving us each a unique part to play in the same shared ministry.

Here are two uncomplicated steps we need to take.

Small Acts of Daily Obedience

"Teacher, which is the greatest commandment in the Law?" Jesus replied: "'Love the Lord your God with all your heart and with all your soul and with all your mind.' This is the first and greatest commandment." Matthew 22:36–38

The simplicity of what Jesus taught during his lifetime is frequently overlooked. Often we long for what some call the deeper teachings of Christ, yet we miss the simple genius of Christ. In reality, the deeper teachings are found by just allowing simple truths to sink further into our hearts and shine light on our motivations. The teaching above is such simple teaching with deep effect. This is what makes it the greatest commandment.

Here's what I mean.

While I may know initially that God wants me to love him with all my heart, soul, and mind, I will spend a lifetime discovering what this really means. Initially, I may believe I love him completely, only to discover after numerous daily failures that there are many places in my life where I continue to resist him. Over time I discover that I have not yet fully loved him with all my heart, soul, and mind. So I must let him love me more fully every day so that I can in turn love him–and others–more fully.

But Jesus does this with everything. He makes everything simple. Even our call to a life of ministry. Here is how Jesus makes that invitation.

> *As Jesus was walking beside the Sea of Galilee, he saw two brothers, Simon called Peter and his brother Andrew. They were casting a net into the lake, for they were fishermen. "Come, follow me," Jesus said, "and I will send you out to fish for people." At once they left their nets and followed him.* Matthew 4:18–20

What men overcomplicate, Jesus makes simple. "Come, follow me." That's it. That is where a life of ministry, good works, and service begins. Jesus calls, and we go with him.

Most men overthink this and make it more complicated. We frequently think we are looking for a calling in an occupational sense, a specialized, ongoing task we can do for God. This is not the case. In fact, it's not our calling at all; Jesus is the one calling. It's a "following" we seek. We are called only to follow. In the following we become more like Christ. Daily we are transformed and fall more in love with him with all our heart, soul, and mind. We steadily subject ourselves to a regular repurposing. This repurposing, initiated by Christ and empowered by the Holy Spirit, works to put to death the ways of the flesh and awakens godly motivation. And it is out of this power that we do daily ministry, good works, and acts of service.

And whatever you do, whether in word or deed, do it all in the name of the Lord Jesus, giving thanks to God the Father through him. Colossians 3:17

This means our ministry is not just another job. While there are people out there who do ministry as a profession, do not be confused—ministry is not a job. Ministry is everything we do by the Spirit. Every word and action should proceed out of that relationship and in furtherance of God's purpose. Many newcomers to the Christian faith will look at paid professional ministers and assume that their training makes them the only ones qualified to do the work. It is easy to draw this assumption, but this is not the right conclusion.

At the root, ministry is an action, not a job and not a title. Just because someone is paid to do ministerial work and bears a title that designates him as a leader within the church, this does not mean that only such people are ministers. Check out what Paul says about this.

So Christ himself gave the apostles, the prophets, the evangelists, the pastors and teachers, to equip his people for works of service, so that the body of Christ may be built up. Ephesians 4:11–12

God's idea of ministry is broad and inclusive. He includes all his people in the work of ministry. That's men like you and me. We are all ministers. In our daily following, we do actions of ministry, or what Paul here calls works of service. And ministry requires daily awareness, daily effort, which is refined by daily challenges. Ministry is learned and developed through daily success and failure in the following of Jesus Christ.

And here's who started it all—our first minister, Jesus Christ.

For the Son of Man came to seek and to save the lost. Luke 19:10

Our response to this is to allow Jesus to minister to us and then reciprocate according to what we receive. We minister because we have been ministered to. When see ministry as an activity, we are subject then to the process.

"If you love me, keep my commands." John 14:15

The one who keeps God's commands lives in him, and he in them. And this is how we know that he lives in us: We know it by the Spirit he gave us. 1 John 3:24

Do not merely listen to the word, and so deceive yourselves. Do what it says. Anyone who listens to the word but does not do what it says is like someone who looks at his face in a mirror and, after looking at himself, goes away and immediately forgets what he looks like. But whoever looks intently into the perfect law that gives freedom, and continues in it—not forgetting what they have heard, but doing it—they will be blessed in what they do. James 1:22–25

When it comes to our ministry, I think we wrestle in contemplation with ourselves too much, which leads to hesitation. We overthink it, desiring too much assurance before we begin. Maybe we thrive on the concrete feeling of some sort of affirmation and self-confidence. But consider this: Did Abraham know that he was going to be called the father of faith when God called him out of Ur? Did David know he was going to be called a man after God's own heart? Neither of these men knew what God would do through them or how they would be remembered–but they acted obediently. They acted like called men. I really don't think they spent much time second-guessing their decision to obey. Even the apostle Paul put it simply: his aim? To complete the task and testify to the good news of God's grace. He was simply obedient: his titles, identity, and all the other peripheral matters developed over time. Through his obedience he became known to us as an author, church consultant, evangelist, apostle, and teacher. But if you worry about titles, you'll start overthinking; and if you do that, you'll end up hesitating.

Here is a personal example. You may quickly identify me as an author or speaker, but strangely it took me years to even call myself by those titles. Why? Well, because I did not see my talents, abilities, and gifts in the same way that God (and others) saw them. I still feel a little awkward embracing these titles. Like you, I can quickly disqualify myself. I think most men do this.

As God's man, you need to worry less about ministry titles and spend more time just being obedient. Take one step at a time, follow God's call, and along the way you may discover a title. Along the way of obedience, you will uncover passions, talents, abilities, and gifts that will routinely advance God's purposes through you to others. Leverage them for kingdom purposes by, in, and through obedience.

Consider this question: How does God want you to follow him in obedience today? Answer this question today, and then act on it. In fact, make this determination each day this week, and the results will encourage you to continue this routine for the rest of your life. As you follow God, you'll discover how he is shaping and naming your calling. You'll be able to look back, amazed at the ministry God has been accomplishing through you, and you might even discover that others will give you titles along the way.

Small Acts of Daily Influence

> *Therefore, my dear brothers and sisters, stand firm. Let nothing move you. Always give yourselves fully to the work of the Lord, because you know that your labor in the Lord is not in vain.* 1 Corinthians 15:58

I believe we underestimate the power of daily influence, by far. When we act with integrity and consistency over a long period of time, our lives can have an extraordinary impact. By standing firm, being immovable, and remaining dedicated to good works, the people around us will be inspired to change their own behavior. Integrity is hard work, but its effects multiply beyond our expectations.

We often miss the chance to exert daily influence because we love the idea of a quick fix, the fast track to high impact. We men will even praise and idolize this short-sighted behavior when we see others successfully use it to get what they want. Yet the long-term simplicity and power of daily influence has compound results. Just ask anyone in finance about the power of compound interest. One thing done regularly over a long period of time has incredible results and can produce sustained impact.

Listen to Paul's words to the Roman believers.

God, whom I serve in my spirit in preaching the gospel of his Son, is my witness how constantly I remember you in my prayers at all times; and I pray that now at last by God's will the way may be opened for me to come to you. I long to see you so that I may impart to you some spiritual gift to make you strong—that is, that you and I may be mutually encouraged by each other's faith. I do not want you to be unaware, brothers and sisters, that I planned many times to come to you (but have been prevented from doing so until now) in order that I might have a harvest among you, just as I have had among the other Gentiles. I am obligated both to Greeks and non-Greeks, both to the wise and the foolish. That is why I am so eager to preach the gospel also to you who are in Rome. For I am not ashamed of the gospel, because it is the power of God that brings salvation to everyone who believes: first to the Jew, then to the Gentile. Romans 1:9–16

I love what Paul does here. It may seem a little less than obvious at first, but he's explaining his ministry as obedience to Christ. He also interjects his desire for continued influence, for an ongoing communal relationship with them. In a heartfelt way, he is referencing his ministry and explaining how badly he wants to do it with them. Here's the breakdown; it's pretty simple.

- Preaching
- Praying
- Planning
- Prevented–for now
- But I'll keep on preaching unashamedly anyway

For Paul this was an easy list. It wasn't rocket science. In fact, we might even say Paul is overly simplistic. It wasn't a title or notoriety he sought with the Roman Christians. He desired to demonstrate obedience, to engage in small steps of hopeful, active influence over a long period of time. He stayed with it until God opened the next door, and then the next, and the next. And because he was unable to be with this congregation in person, he persisted. He extended his ministry influence by writing a long letter to them that we know as the book of Romans–one of the most influential books of the Bible. His letter not only reached the people of Rome, it reaches us today.

I am sure Paul had no idea that this prevention of influence was going to result in even greater influence for the kingdom.

I am sure Paul had no idea that this momentary prevention of influence was going to result in even greater influence for the kingdom. Paul's wish was to preach to them in person, but God knew the letter would have far greater influence over time. While Paul worried that God's plan might be thwarted, God instead led him down an even more influential path for not only Rome, but also planet Earth. But Paul had to take that next small step in lieu of the one he had anticipated.

Sometimes it's the small steps that matter the most. Paul was a master of understanding this type of influence: one small step of influence daily.

Paul maintained influence by taking a small step in lieu of the ones he had wanted to take.

As a man of God, you need to see the opportunity you have to influence the people around you. You already have a number of circles of influence at this present moment. Here are four primary circles of influence of every man: home, work, neighbors, and friends. There are people within your reach every day. God has given you these circles and the people within them, and you need to minister to them first. This is your circle of influence. Frequently we overlook them, but we should not. They are our first ministry.

> *"Hear, O Israel: The Lord our God, the Lord is one. Love the Lord your God with all your heart and with all your soul and with all your strength. These commandments that I give you today are to be on your hearts. Impress them on your children. Talk about them when you sit at home and when you walk along the road, when you lie down and when you get up. Tie them as symbols on your hands and bind them on your foreheads. Write them on the doorframes of your houses and on your gates."* Deuteronomy 6:4–9

These words stand out tall among the Old Testament scriptures. God knows that a man who is obedient first to God and who leverages that obedience to influence those around him will change himself, his home, his family, his nation, and his culture over time. So much potential lays within a single man who aligns himself with God and then influences others along the way. Think first of the ones you talk, sit, walk, lie, and get up with at home. Here is where your influence will primarily be felt. You need to understand the power of small acts of daily influence.

We sometimes forget that we have a wife to lead, children to disciple, employees to guide, and neighbors to serve. Living in godly obedience to them is where we begin; we must daily influence them in small steps over a long period of time. Remember, your ministry will not take shape overnight. But it won't take shape at all unless you do the daily work required.

So Now Put It Together

So now to give it punch, we have to do some assembly.

Obedience + Influence = Maximum Impact

As we live obediently, we will naturally exert our influence. For example, let's say that my step of obedience today is to "speak more kindly to my family." This single act of obedience, done daily, can have a huge impact on others, but we underestimate its influence. So, convicted by my careless words, I decide to hold a family meeting after dinner. Speaking first to my wife in front of my children, I say something like this:

> *"I have come to realize that lately I have been coming home stressed out by the challenges at work and have been taking some of this out on each of you. First, I want you each to know I am sorry, and second, I am going to work to speak more kindly to each of you."*

This is a statement of confession and repentance that communicates my spiritual conviction and models obedience to God. Most of the time, we will make these statements privately, but sometimes we have to go public. By publicly addressing mistakes, we make our obedience visible to all. We don't do it to put on a show, but rather to demonstrate humility and put ourselves under accountability. This is spiritual leadership of the self.

But taking this one step further, we can appropriately leverage this moment to influence others. I could also add this:

> *"I have also noticed that this has affected how you each speak to one another. And I am not happy about this. We need to find better ways to interact with one another. So I want you to join me in speaking more kindly to each other. Let's focus on being positive and uplifting and using a more positive tone with each other in the house."*

Now that's influence. It could be a directional moment that changes a family forever. Your wife and kids will never forget it. First, because it is honest and self-revealing about your desire to be more obedient. Second, because you used that moment to teach and influence them toward a different way of life. Now imagine a lifetime of moments like this with your family. Can you imagine engaging in a more powerful ministry? But that's the teaching of Deuteronomy 6.

Now do the same not only at home, but also at work and with friends and neighbors as God allows. Do the same in your daily interaction with people, but keep it even simpler and speed it up.

Hey John. Yesterday at work I came down kind of hard on you. I just wanted to tell you I reflected on how I handled that, and this morning I felt convicted, and I want to apologize. Just know I am working on this, and I want to find better ways to interact.

So Coach, at practice yesterday I felt like we handled things poorly. I was thinking and even praying about it this morning, and I would like to help build a different spirit on our team. Is there something I can do?

Stacey, I noticed yesterday you were having a hard day. Is there something I can pray about for you today?

This is ministry. It's ministry that only you can do. When you follow Jesus it results in influence, yet we take it for granted all the time. We should not hesitate to act on it, and to act on it frequently.

We need to remember the subsequent actions that follow. It's obedience plus added influence. The manner in which we obey, the character by which we obey, and the spiritual application we make while obeying determine how much influence we exert. So, as I speak more kindly to everyone in my household, the manner, character, and spiritual application I make is how I influence my family for the kingdom. It has power to change us and others around us–forever.

Obedience results in influence.

Men, we underestimate the spiritual influence we have. Maybe we see our world with our natural sight. But we should see the world spiritually. You are not merely a plumber, builder, construction worker, designer, leader, consultant, speaker, writer, composer, advisor, or administrator. There is a spiritual reality behind each of these roles. The title you actually bear is far weightier than all of these, and it informs your spiritual identity. You are a servant of Christ. This title is greater than the sum of all these roles put together. Fellas, you are each a servant of the Most High God. Everything else is secondary–even that occupation that you hold in high regard. While today we may be plumbing, building, constructing, designing, leading, consulting, speaking, writing, and administrating, we are first a servant to Christ. I think this is why so many of the New Testament writers state this title with such prevalence. Note their self-proclaimed titles:

Paul, a servant of Christ Jesus (Romans 1:1)
Simon Peter, a servant and apostle of Jesus Christ (2 Peter 1:1)
James, a servant of God and of the Lord Jesus Christ. (James 1:1)
Jude, a servant of Jesus Christ (Jude 1)
His servant John (Revelation 1:1)

Yet as Christian men, God gives us redemptive power over his creation. This is done as God's servant. This is our primary identity. While others may interpret us through natural titles, these titles take a radical second place in our life. Like Peter, who was once a fisherman, then transformed into a fisher of men. Like Paul, who was once a persecutor of Christians, then transformed into a preacher to the nations. Our seemingly natural abilities are far more useful when wielded in service to God. We can redeem activities that appear outright profane.

For example, take crucifixion. Crucifixion was a very real method of execution, and it was horrific. But the character of Jesus, the manner in which he died, and the spiritual application he made while being crucified turned a devastating moment into something with supernatural consequences that still echoes across the world today. And Jesus did this in hopes that we would watch and do the same. Even activities that are frequently used for horrific evil can be redeemed for godly purpose.

But gentlemen, we have to come to terms with our big ideas about ministry. Big ideas can become a big idol. Just as God can redeem the profane for his purposes, we can soil what ought to be sacred. I confess I want to have a big influence during my lifetime. I do. But any idea of big ministry can be motivated by selfish intent. Ministry is something God does through all of us, not one of us. Ministry is not a stage for our fame;

it's God plan for worldwide redemption. We all play a role, we must carry it out via small acts over a long period of time, and God is responsible for the big results–and he gets to keep all the glory. Don't become mesmerized with big ministry and miss the power of your small influence done daily.

Do this today: consider how God might want to use you to affect your circles of influence on this particular day. Consider the four circles of influence mentioned above–home, work, friends, and neighbors. Then name the people within your circle of influence that you need to serve in active obedience. And then act. Influence them through your obedience. And then repeat that tomorrow, and then the next day, and so on.

Your character (who you are), your manner (the way you act), and your voice (what you say as you act) have a transformational impact on others. This happens naturally. Once your character, manner, and voice are redeemed by God, and then used for his purposes, they, too, will become tools for godly influence.

> *I long to see you so that I may impart to you some spiritual gift to make you strong—that is, that you and I may be mutually encouraged by each other's faith.* Romans 1:11–12

Reflection & Discussion Questions

1. When you think about the word "ministry" what image comes to mind?
2. Describe a moment in your life that God used you to do ministry.
3. How do you think God would describe your unique purpose?
4. Have you ever disqualified yourself from doing ministry? What was your reason for this personal disqualification?

Call to Action

The following steps are your call to action in the area of ministry.

Activate Ministry:

- **Small Acts of Daily Obedience:** How are you being called to be obedient today? Write it down.
- **Small Acts of Daily Influence:** How might you use this act of obedience to influence others? Write it down.

If you want help stepping through ministry, consider following along with me on the **35-Day Challenge** that pairs with this book. Check it out online at www.beresolute.org/called-to-act

CONCLUSION

How to Build a Movement

What if we could start a movement of men? Imagine a groundswell rising up and sweeping the nation, even the world, as men respond to Jesus's call. Imagine a new season of man marked not by apathy, but obedient action.

I meet men with this type of passion all the time. They are longing to start a movement of men in their church, in their community, and far beyond.

But get this: there are already thousands of these mini-movements for men all over the world. And most of them are small. Some of them focus on adventure, some on retreats, some on conferences, and some on discipleship. Whatever their focus, each lays claim to the issue at hand, calling men to act.

I want you to notice the operative word here: small.

Men, we are a small part of a sprawling and very disorganized movement, but don't fail to see the ingenuity in this.

The timeless means of preparing men to hear and act has been accomplished through one-on-one relationships or the men's small group. Perhaps you've been a part of a mentoring group, leadership group, or discipleship group. The name is irrelevant, though many people get hung up on defining these groups because they think they have "the sauce" that others do not. But they are just groups, no matter what you dub them. We should be concerned about the outcomes.

Within these simple one-on-one relationships, triads, or small groups we have the opportunity to change the world. Yes, the world. Our seemingly insignificant gatherings are frequently overlooked because we do not have the flair of a big, thriving, engaging, and attractive men's ministry. But small, intimate groups could be the best choice for building a worldwide movement. This method has been tested, and guess what? It works.

Here's evidence.

2,000 years ago, Jesus gathered twelve previously unnoticed men: Thomas; Simon the Zealot; Philip; Simon Peter; Matthew; Jude; Judas Iscariot; John; James, son of Alpheus; James, son of Zebedee; Bartholomew; and Andrew. These men were called at different times and had a variety of life experiences and professional skills. Jesus invested a mere 2-3 years into these men from the moment he called the first one until his death on the cross. And in this time, this small group of men learned how to hear and act and help the world to hear and act. In fact, you are reading this book today because of what Jesus invested into these twelve men 2,000 years ago. Through the repetition of regular activities, Jesus developed men called to act.

There's no doubt that some noteworthy things can happen in massive gatherings and in large events, but effective transmission of gospel and manhood does not.

Remember the end game: it's helping men to hear and to act. They need guidance tailored specifically to them along the way. Had "mass mentorship" worked, Jesus would have done it. But even he, the King of Glory, didn't do it this way.

So Build a Movement

Again, don't overcomplicate this. It's quite simple. Movements begin small and with the faithful obedience of a few. Start with a smaller group, and just do these three things (and only these three things). Don't add to it and don't take from it.

The Men

The first thing you need to do is select some men. Jesus did the same thing. He went out and selected twelve guys. They were men he had a connection with; men he felt would benefit the movement in a variety of ways. He didn't put an ad in the church program or make an announcement from the platform; he went out into the world and selected the men he wanted. He didn't plan a men's event, build an infrastructure, or even build a multi-layered business plan. If you want to start a movement, this is where it begins: with you inviting one man. And then another. And then another.

There is not a lot of ingenuity that goes into selecting your own men. In a way, you get everything you select. So go get the men of the age, demographic, maturity, and challenges you want to reach. You are able to select the ones you think will be the most responsive to your leadership. And since this is exactly what Jesus did, let's just do that.

But here is the one qualifier I would keep in mind when selecting your men. I would look for men who are hungry. Not physical hunger, because every man is physically hungry. Instead, seek out spiritually hungry men; each man you select should have some form of spiritual hunger. It's Jesus's ultimate qualifier. With these words Jesus called his twelve men: "Come follow me." Then those who were spiritually hungry left everything and joined his group. The first Christian group. Christ's group.

Now it's your turn. Scratch down 1 to 12 men you would select (yes, it's okay to have less than 12):

The Meeting

The second thing you need to do to start a movement is determine your meeting time and location. This is not rocket science, but it's a critical step.

I would select a time and location that works for you and then invite the other men to it. Tell them where you are going to be and when you are going to be there, and they will come if they can. It's really quite simple. If you waver on this one, the men you've invited will immediately determine you are not organized and prepared. As leader and organizer, your presence is critical, so make sure that whatever schedule you set will work for you most of the time.

You'll want to accommodate to some degree, but when we overaccommodate, men smell weakness, and they will not follow. Jesus was strong, not soft on this. "Come follow me" indicates a departure from doing life as it has been; you're meeting with Jesus on his terms and his time. So why do something different?

Now it's your turn. Write down some meeting times that work for you:

The Material

If there is one thing that is complicated, it's this question: "What should we study or talk about when we get together?" I understand why men feel this way. There are all kinds of curricula on the market today. We're swimming in an ocean of content. Combine this with the fact that men are coming from a variety of backgrounds, with a variety of issues, and a variety of spiritual maturities.

I've got an idea! Let's ditch the curriculum altogether, and let's just use the Bible. Just build five fundamentals into men: prayer, scripture, brotherhood, accountability, and ministry. And then let's practice these fundamentals repeatedly and watch what God does. After all, this was Jesus's model of spiritual leadership.

We need to think more simply about this. We don't need more material than the Bible. We don't need a complicated scope and sequence to spiritual development. Men just need to hear and act, so let's support that process.

Structure a small group around the five fundamentals covered in this book. If you need an outline, do this:

- **PRAYER** (5 minutes): As a group, ask for prayer requests and then, using the P.A.C.T. method, pray.
- **SCRIPTURE** (20 minutes): As a group, select a paragraph or section of scripture and study it using the P.A.S.S. method.
- **BROTHERHOOD** (15 minutes): In pairs, use the 411-of-Brotherhood method to have a discussion.
- **ACCOUNTABILITY** (10 minutes): In pairs, practice D.O. accountability.
- **MINISTRY** (10 minutes): As a group, talk about one man's ministry talents, abilities, and gifts and learn how he used them over the last week.

Are You All In?

Gentlemen, I am looking for men to lead groups just like these. It doesn't matter if you have one man, twelve men, or a hundred men. By answering God's call and taking action alongside just one other believer, you become part of the largest, most widespread movement in the world. The world overlooks our men's groups, but who cares? We are men led by God, instructed by Christ, and guided by the Holy Spirit. Do not underestimate the power of your small, decentralized cell (or tribe, or group) within the movement. You may be few, but that doesn't change the impact God can have through your actions. Remember, God is unleashed by faithful action, not your personal follower count. So join the movement. God's movement. And go all in.

> *And whatever you do, whether in word or deed, do it all in the name of the Lord Jesus, giving thanks to God the Father through him.*
> Colossians 3:17

> *Then Jesus said to his disciples, "Whoever wants to be my disciple must deny themselves and take up their cross and follow me. For whoever wants to save their life will lose it, but whoever loses their life for me will find it. What good will it be for someone to gain the whole world, yet forfeit their soul? Or what can anyone give in exchange for their soul?* Matthew 16:24–26

If you are a leading a group, I would love to hear about your adventures. You can call, text, or email anytime:

Vince Miller | 651-274-8796 | vince@beresolute.org | www.beresolute.org

THE MEN'S DAILY DEVO

Check out the *Men's Daily Devotional* — it's short, sweet, and to the point. You can find it right on the home page of our website at beresolute.org, or just go to mensdevo.org.

CALLED TO ACT

5 Session Video-Led Bible Study

On the Resolute website, get access to the 5-session study that equips men in the five disciplines contained in part two of this book. Vince Miller will lead you and the men you lead through an interactive and engaging study that motivates men to weave these disciplines into the every pattern of their life. Check it out and all Resolute small group materials at www.beresolute.org